FINDING JOY
in EVERY
SEASON

In *Finding Joy in Every Season*, Chris Corradino successfully sheds light on God's thoughts in a fresh, new way. Through his journey with the Lord, he has revealed profound insight that is applicable to men seeking transformation. Readers will unlock actionable wisdom for God to move in their own lives.

—Ryan Sims, Pastor
Equippers Church, Napier, New Zealand

In his book *Finding Joy in Every Season*, Chris has chosen to not just open his heart and share his journey and trials but to also open his life thus far for our benefit. With skillful creativity, Chris infuses words and Scripture that remind and encourage readers of the potential of hope and therefore the potential for change. As Chris shares and reflects on the all-too-real struggle of our reality, his book ushers us from the place of challenge and proposes a Christ-centered solution. If you are looking for a fresh and relevant dose of encouragement and Scripture, I would highly recommend you getting yourself a copy.

—Peter Brothers, Pastor
Equippers Church, Hastings, New Zealand

60 Men's Devotionals for Winning with Jesus

Finding Joy in Every Season

Chris Corradino

Ambassador International
Greenville, South Carolina & Belfast, Northern Ireland
www.ambassador-international.com

FINDING JOY IN EVERY SEASON
60 Men's Devotionals for Winning with Jesus
©2024 by Chris Corradino
All rights reserved

Hardcover ISBN: 978-1-64960-505-4
Paperback ISBN: 978-1-64960-506-1
eISBN: 978-1-64960-549-8

No part of this publication may be reproduced, distributed, or transmitted in any form or by any means, including photocopying, recording, or other electronic or mechanical methods, without the prior written permission of the publisher, except in the case of brief quotations embodied in critical reviews and certain other noncommercial uses permitted by copyright law. For permission requests, contact the publisher using the information below.

Cover design by Hannah Linder Designs
Interior typesetting by Dentelle Design

Scripture quotations are taken from the *Holy Bible*, New Living Translation, copyright © 1996, 2004, 2015 by Tyndale House Foundation. Used by permission of Tyndale House Publishers, Inc., Carol Stream, Illinois 60188. All rights reserved.

Ambassador International books may be purchased in bulk for education, business, fundraising, or sales promotional use. For information, please email sales@emeraldhouse.com.

AMBASSADOR INTERNATIONAL	AMBASSADOR BOOKS
Emerald House	The Mount
411 University Ridge, Suite B14	2 Woodstock Link
Greenville, SC 29601	Belfast, BT6 8DD
United States	Northern Ireland, United Kingdom
www.ambassador-international.com	www.ambassadormedia.co.uk

The colophon is a trademark of Ambassador, a Christian publishing company.

To my wife, whose unwavering love and encouragement have opened my eyes to the potential God placed in my life and in our family

To my sons, who often reveal the heart of God with their childlike innocence and innate wisdom

To my mom, who modeled what it looks like to walk with steadfast faith in Jesus even through difficult times

To my brother and sister, who have been lifelong friends, confidants, and pillars of strength

To my late father, who taught me about the power of prayer

To my late daughter, whose life and passing inspired this book, brought our family closer together, and showed me how God can use all things for the greater good

Table of Contents

Introduction   13

1
The Gift of Grief   15

2
Softer   17

3
The Power of Tears   19

4
Seeing Red   21

5
Exceeding Your Baggage Limit   23

6
Failing Religiously   25

7
The Weight of What If   27

8
Be the Sequoia Tree   29

9
Mental Health Matters   33

10
Scars That Go Unseen   35

11
THE GOSPEL OF PEACE   39

12
WHAT DEATH TEACHES
US ABOUT LIFE   41

13
SEEKING EXTRA HELP   45

14
THE ARCHITECT OF YOUR LIFE   47

15
THE COLORFUL LENS OF JESUS   49

16
THE BEST WAY TO
HEAR GOD'S VOICE   51

17
WAITING ON GOD TO DELIVER   55

18
BIBLE BEFORE BREAKING NEWS   57

19
GOD IN THE UNEXPECTED   59

20
ACCESSING GOD'S PRAYER SUPPORT (GPS)   61

21
FIRST AID FAITH   63

22
LIFTING THE BIBLE   65

23
THE ULTIMATE HOW-TO GOD   69

24
WHAT BRINGS US TOGETHER? 71

25
I WILL PRAY FOR YOU 75

26
THE LOGIC OF GOD IS LOVE 77

27
CONFRONTED BY JESUS 79

28
MEANT TO LOVE 81

29
WHEN THE LUSTER FADES 83

30
PUTTING THE CONTEXT BACK INTO SEX 87

31
DO IT WITHOUT GRIPING 91

32
CAUGHT IN THE ACT 95

33
LET JESUS BE THE GOALIE 97

34
FAMILY IS NOT A WEAKNESS 99

35
A FORK IN THE ROAD 103

36
RESTRUCTURING THE ORG CHART 107

37
COLLABORATING WITH GOD 109

38
THE RECOVERING PEOPLE-PLEASER 111

39
ACCEPTING PRAISE GRACEFULLY 115

40
CALLING TIME-OUT 117

41
SIGNS AND WONDERS 119

42
WHAT HAS GOD DONE FOR ME LATELY? 121

43
BEING CHOSEN 125

44
IT IS NOT THE SIZE THAT MATTERS 127

45
WRESTLING WITH GOD 131

46
GAINING CONTROL BY LETTING GO 133

47
FUELED BY GOD 137

48
GETTING STARTED 139

49
SHIELDED BY SCRIPTURE 143

50
POSITIONED FOR SUCCESS 145

51
SHAME UNMASKED 147

52

WHEN QUITTING IS ESSENTIAL   149

53

CONTROLLED BURNS   151

54

FROM HANDCUFFS TO PRAISE   155

55

SPIRITUAL BOOT CAMP   157

56

RELATIONSHIP OVER RELIGION   159

57

EXERCISING FAITH IN THE FACE OF DOUBT   163

58

DROPPING CRUISE CONTROL   165

59

WHEN BAD NEWS COMES   167

60

JESUS NEVER FAILS   169

ABOUT THE AUTHOR   171

*So we must listen very carefully to the truth we have heard,
or we may drift away from it.*

—Hebrews 2:1

Introduction

WHEN MY WIFE ABBIE AND I unexpectedly lost our baby girl Joy as a twenty-one-week stillborn, I was brought to my knees. It was not to pray but rather to cry and agonize over the pain. Sure, I talked with God, but it was mostly to ask why He would allow such a tragedy to occur.

In the days that followed, the midwife and hospital staff were diligent about checking on my wife's well-being. I was so glad she was receiving this necessary support but also surprised at the absence of any protocol in relation to men. And while I may not have physically carried or delivered our baby, my heart and mind were still ravaged by grief.

I searched the web and found scores of dads who were experiencing the same disparity. Continued research led me to a jaw-dropping statistic from a 2022 CDC report. It showed that the overall suicide rate in America had increased by 30 percent between 2000 and 2020. During this same period, the number of males ending their lives tragically was three to four times higher than women.[1] Whether

---

[1] Matthew F. Garnett, Sally C. Curtin, and Deborah M. Stone, "Suicide mortality in the United States, 2000–2020," NCHS Data Brief, No. 433 (March 2022): Hyattsville, MD: National Center for Health Statistics, https://www.cdc.gov/nchs/products/databriefs/db433.htm.

this resulted from limited resources available to men, the stigma of asking for help, or both, the need is clear.

If we want to see real change, the battles that rage within us can no longer be hidden from view. For men who have long been taught to lead with strength, the concepts presented in this book may sometimes feel counterintuitive. In the ultimate of plot twists, it is in our weakest moments that God unleashes His mighty power. It was in this place of desperation that Jesus met me and revealed how to live with abundant joy once again. His wisdom is spread across the pages of this devotional.

So, is cultivating happiness feasible amid our darkest seasons? Jesus tells us that with God, nothing is impossible (Matt. 19:26). My prayer is that these pages will open your heart just enough for Jesus to move in and transform your life in profound ways.

1

The Gift of Grief

WHETHER WE LAY OUR DEAD to rest in a cemetery or have them cremated, the symbolism is quite similar. We cover the casket with soil or put a lid on the urn. Life marches on, and we end up burying our emotions just to keep in step. In this, we inadvertently trample on our grief rather than support it. This inhospitable environment stifles any chance for healing to grow.

This is not to suggest that we mummify those who die and leave them on display. Yet we also should not keep our grieving under wraps. Some experts claim that you need to walk through a five-stage process. While this makes for an interesting read, our grief does not coincide with the tidy chapters of a book. Every loss is different, except for one constant truth: Jesus is closest to the brokenhearted.

Expressing your sorrow will be painful, but suppressing it can ravage your soul. In reflecting on the loss, you make space for God to reveal how to best use it. At first, you may need to scream, punch a heavy bag, write about it, toss rose petals into the ocean, or listen to sad music and cry. Over time, a new chapter starts to emerge in which you can honor with your actions those who have passed on.

This devotional book, for example, arose from the crushing loss of our baby Joy. In grief counseling, as well as in time spent studying God's Word, I stopped asking why and began to accept His will. Yes, it still hurts, but the Bible details how even the most painful death of Jesus' crucifixion was used for the greater good of the world. I do not pretend to have all the answers, but I do have peace stemming from God's grace.

KEY THOUGHT: The death of a loved one is a heavy cross to bear. Instead of carrying it on your own, draw close to God, Who comforts all who suffer.

ADDITIONAL READING:
- "So you have sorrow now, but I will see you again; then you will rejoice, and no one can rob you of that joy" (John 16:22).
- "The Lord is close to the brokenhearted; he rescues those whose spirits are crushed" (Psalm 34:18).
- "When you go through deep waters, I will be with you. When you go through rivers of difficulty, you will not drown. When you walk through the fire of oppression, you will not be burned up; the flames will not consume you."
- "'Do not be afraid or discouraged, for the Lord will personally go ahead of you. He will be with you; he will neither fail you nor abandon you'" (Deut. 31:8).

2

Softer

MEN'S FAITH CONFERENCES AROUND THE globe typically come with bold taglines that boast a call to arms. Some are labeled with powerful names such as "Stronger" or "Soldier On." But while the overarching mission of these events is positive, they often miss the understated power of vulnerability. In fairness to the marketing teams who promote these gatherings, would anyone show up to an event with a name like "Softer"?

Therein lies the tension plaguing men from all walks of life. Jesus calls us to exercise humility rather than focus on vain ambition. He teaches us to turn the other cheek as opposed to hitting back. Society, on the other hand, glorifies those who can quickly steamroll their opponent and cause them to tap out.

In many instances, though, we are fighting the demons within. All the muscles in the world cannot soothe the hurt we carry inside. While it sounds counterintuitive, brawn starts with embracing our weaknesses.

So, how do we reconcile this with God? Start by asking yourself whose playbook you are following. If it is the ideals dictated by popular culture, you are setting yourself up for failure. Just as a bodybuilder's physique eventually fades, so do the trends many use to identify themselves.

On the contrary, God's faithfulness never changes. What may be viewed as a shortcoming will be used to redeem your past and bring glory to His name. It is in this process we find that true strength does not come from us but from Him.

Key Thought: Lay your weapons down, for Jesus has already claimed the victory.

Additional Reading:
- "Humble yourselves before the Lord, and he will lift you up in honor" (James 4:10).
- "That's why I take pleasure in my weaknesses, and in the insults, hardships, persecutions, and troubles that I suffer for Christ. For when I am weak, then I am strong" (2 Cor. 12:10).
- "God is my strong fortress, and he makes my way perfect. He makes me as surefooted as a deer, enabling me to stand on mountain heights. He trains my hands for battle; he strengthens my arm to draw a bronze bow" (2 Sam. 22:33-35).
- "'I have told you all this so that you may have peace in me. Here on earth you will have many trials and sorrows. But take heart, because I have overcome the world'" (John 16:33).

3
The Power of Tears

DURING HIS TIME ON EARTH, Jesus was fully God and yet entirely Man. He experienced the suffering and sadness of the human condition just as we do today. Whether it was anguish over the lost souls of Jerusalem, the death of His friend Lazarus, or the extreme pain He was to physically endure, Jesus had a deep understanding of sorrow. So how did this Man, Who also carried the Divine power of God, deal with all of this? Put simply, "Jesus wept" (John 11:35).

In three passages of revealing Scripture (Luke 19:41, John 11:35, Heb. 5:7-9), we learn that Jesus did not just shed a few tears and have a back-slapping, "hug it out, bro" moment. Instead, He sobbed unabashedly while others looked on. Here was God in the flesh modeling what it looks like to be a man.

This may take some by surprise as modern society often depicts crying as a lack of strength, particularly for men. Even dramatic movies considered to be tearjerkers are often dubbed as "chick flicks." As a result, we turn off the lights and watch in a dark room to hide our tears. Yet the moving topics these films explore have universal appeal, regardless of gender. When we stow away our emotions in shame, it creates the perfect breeding ground for the enemy to sow weeds of sabotage.

In looking at Jesus' example, we gain new insight on how to best process our feelings. By openly expressing His emotions, Jesus showed what researchers would discover thousands of years later. Crying releases natural chemicals that ease the pain of both physical and emotional distress. When we use this God-given gift, it will not only help us feel better but also draw us closer to Him.

KEY THOUGHT: Jesus was all-powerful, and His tears are an example of how crying is a position of strength. In showing your emotions, you become more like Him and the man you were called to be.

ADDITIONAL READING:
- "While Jesus was here on earth, he offered prayers and pleadings, with a loud cry and tears, to the one who could rescue him from death. And God heard his prayers because of his deep reverence for God" (Heb. 5:7).
- "But as he came closer to Jerusalem and saw the city ahead, he began to weep" (Luke 19:41).
- "When Jesus saw her weeping and saw the other people wailing with her, a deep anger welled up within him, and he was deeply troubled. 'Where have you put him?' he asked them. They told him, 'Lord, come and see.' Then Jesus wept (John 11:33-35).
- "For, There is one God and one Mediator who can reconcile God and humanity—the man Christ Jesus" (1 Tim. 2:5).

SEEING RED

MAYBE IT IS THE KIDS who seem to have a knack for pushing your buttons. Perhaps you had an argument with your spouse, or were disrespected by the boss, or received a less-than-flattering comment from a family member. These can all raise our temperatures and leave us hot under the collar. In some instances, we lose our cool and say things of which we are not proud. If we truly repent and ask God for forgiveness, it will be granted.

Yet how can we ensure the same pattern will not play out again? Despite our best efforts, the conflict will rear its ugly head once more. When it does, what is to stop us from another angry response?

The Bible tells us that real change is steeped in action more so than in good intentions. We need a tried-and-true system to de-escalate before chaos ensues. This method will be different for everyone. The trick is to find the one that works best for you. Some guys find that walking away or doing some kind of physical activity helps.

For me, the most reliable way has been through prayer. In these heightened moments, I will get on my knees, bend over in half, and tell God how angry I am. While I am not proud to admit it, these prayers are quite heated and not always God-honoring. I apologize for this straightaway but explain that I am just furious and need His help. If I am at fault, I confess it. If someone wronged me, I ask for help to forgive them and for the wisdom to see things from all sides. Then I become quiet and just lie in silence. If more anger surfaces, I will continue to pray until, eventually, there is peace.

It is only at this point that I can communicate with the other person involved. More often than not, I am able to humble myself and have a productive discussion. I will ask how I can help move forward and forgive them for what they have done. It is important to note that none of this is predicated on them admitting fault or apologizing to me. Afterward, I may still be disappointed that the conflict occurred in the first place, but if a better path forward has been forged with God, then it was not in vain.

KEY THOUGHT: Anger is a God-given emotion of which we should not automatically dismiss or be ashamed. It is what we do with heightened feelings that ultimately determines their value.

ADDITIONAL READING:
- "But don't just listen to God's word. You must do what it says. Otherwise, you are only fooling yourselves" (James 1:22).
- "A hot-tempered person starts fights; a cool-tempered person stops them" (Prov. 15:18).
- "Fathers, do not provoke your children to anger by the way you treat them. Rather, bring them up with the discipline and instruction that comes from the Lord" (Eph. 6:4).
- "And 'don't sin by letting anger control you.' Don't let the sun go down while you are still angry, for anger gives a foothold to the devil" (Eph. 4:26-27).

Exceeding Your Baggage Limit

HAVE YOU EVER ARRIVED AT the airport with tightly packed suitcases only to be told you have exceeded the weight limit? If you are lucky and one bag is lighter, you can shuffle items around to distribute the weight more evenly. It is when all the luggage is maxed out that you have a real problem.

The same is true in life. What do you do when your stress levels exceed what your soul can handle? For some, we turn to unhealthy indulgences as coping mechanisms. Others choose to over-exercise, immerse themselves in work, and sometimes withdraw from the world around them. These reactions may not appear problematic from afar but are dangerous habits which not only harm our health but also leave little space for God to work.

There is only one solution, and it is not paying for extra cargo. We need to unburden ourselves by transferring the weight to God. There is no need to feel guilty about it as He specifically instructs us to do so. Jesus does not want us to be so anxious that we cannot function. Throughout the Bible, He talks about the importance of resting in His love. That all sounds good on paper, but putting it into practice requires a skill set many of us have not yet mastered.

The first step is to pray about all the things you are juggling. It may even be helpful to write them out. After they are off your chest, ask God for the specific resolutions you would like to see. It is not wrong to make your preferences known to God. He already knows what is on in your mind, so do not be timid. Once the problem is in God's hands, you have the unique opportunity to let it go. In doing this, you are placing trust in Him to work things out in ways that only He can do. Chances are, the solutions will be far superior to anything we could have imagined.

Key Thought: What baggage are you carrying that is preventing you from embracing your true identity? In times of extreme stress, lighten your load by trusting God to carry you through.

Additional Reading:

- "Don't worry about anything; instead, pray about everything. Tell God what you need, and thank him for all he has done" (Phil. 4:6).
- "The Lord replied, 'I will personally go with you, Moses, and I will give you rest—everything will be fine for you'" (Exod. 33:14).
- "Jesus responded, 'Why are you afraid? You have so little faith!' Then he got up and rebuked the wind and waves, and suddenly there was a great calm" (Matt. 8:26).
- "Can all your worries add a single moment to your life" (Luke 12:25).

6
Failing Religiously

IS IT POSSIBLE TO OFTEN fail and still enjoy the favor of God? If the dreams in your heart were placed there by Him, they are worth pursuing, despite the absence of any guarantee. To discern if your goals line up with His will, start by questioning the possible outcome. Should the effort fail, will you consider it time well-spent honoring God or a wasted effort? Nothing you do to glorify Him will be without fruit. Even missing the original target will prove valuable for the greater good of His kingdom.

If you fear failure, it is a revealing indication that your plan is misguided. Efforts that are primarily based on boosting your perceived value are self-serving and therefore not of God. These may have the potential for financial success and renown but come with all the trappings of earthly desires. If the plan does not unfold the way you envisioned it, your self-worth will suffer. Through this, we are reminded that our true identity cannot be found apart from the One Who created us.

The truth is, you may very well be unqualified for the call on your heart. Yet if it is God's plan, He will enable you to strive forward successfully. Why settle for a life of security if it does not increase your reliance on Him? Consider your pursuit a living sacrifice, and the risk of failure will be superseded by a deeper connection with Jesus. This is not to suggest that breaking out of your comfort zone will be easy. Yet any goal that is grounded in glorifying God will be blessed.

The only failure, then, is lacking the faith required to give it your all. Big dreams require unwavering trust and a faithful reliance upon the Lord. Even if you miss the target, you end up in a better place than where your journey started.

KEY THOUGHT: You will know your dream is God-inspired when pride is no longer a disqualifying factor. Step out in faith and fulfill your true calling.

ADDITIONAL READING:
- "'Soon I will die, going the way of everything on earth. Deep in your hearts you know that every promise of the Lord your God has come true. Not a single one has failed!'" (Josh. 23:14).
- "So I say, let the Holy Spirit guide your lives. Then you won't be doing what your sinful nature craves" (Gal. 5:16).
- "'Praise the Lord who has given rest to his people Israel, just as he promised. Not one word has failed of all the wonderful promises he gave through his servant Moses. May the Lord our God be with us as he was with our ancestors; may he never leave us or abandon us'" (1 Kings 8:56-57).
- "Uzziah sought God during the days of Zechariah, who taught him to fear God. And as long as the king sought guidance from the Lord, God gave him success" (2 Chron. 26:5).

7
THE WEIGHT OF WHAT IF

"WHAT IF IT IS CANCER and the kids are forced to grow up without their mother?" "How will I support the family if we lose the house?" "Who will be willing to help us if it all goes downhill?" "When will the constant wave of challenges give way to calm waters?" "Where will I end up if it all comes crashing down?" "Why is God letting all of this happen?" These are actual questions I have pondered, but they are likely not all that different from thoughts you have wrestled.

When our sense of security, purpose, and acceptance is under attack, our perspective becomes rather shortsighted. We know deep down that it is preferable to remain calm and trust God, but our fight-or-flight instinct tugs at us in an unrelenting fashion. How, then, can we find peace in the waiting room of life's most challenging moments? Ironically enough, the answer comes in the form of a question: what if God uses all these situations to fulfill a greater purpose than we can currently grasp?

Now, you have an important choice to make. You can ruminate on anxious thoughts and search the web for solutions, or you can be proactive and pray. If you choose the latter, do not stop with just your prayer. Rally support from your church community as well. Let them know what the problem is and what you are hoping God will do. This helpful step allows them to walk alongside you, lift you up, and maybe even drop off dinner by the house in a pinch. This is the way out of isolation, fear, and the trappings of a negative mind.

When you suffer in silence, the enemy finds ample space to breed discontent. He comes to plunder, poison, and tear down all you have built with God's help. Rather than focusing on what could go wrong, hold firmly to the Lord's promise to see you through. It does not mean things will not come apart at first, but He will use the pieces to build something even more beautiful in the end.

KEY THOUGHT: Do not allow dark thoughts to hold you prisoner in your mind. Interrupt the negative cycle by praying for God's unfailing love and compassion to cover you.

ADDITIONAL READING:
- "'What is the price of five sparrows—two copper coins? Yet God does not forget a single one of them. And the very hairs on your head are all numbered. So don't be afraid; you are more valuable to God than a whole flock of sparrows'" (Luke 12:6-7).
- "What you ought to say is, 'If the Lord wants us to, we will live and do this or that'" (James 4:15).
- "Don't be afraid, for I am with you. Don't be discouraged, for I am your God. I will strengthen you and help you. I will hold you up with my victorious right hand" (Isa. 41:10).
- "You will keep in perfect peace all who trust in you, all whose thoughts are fixed on you" (Isa. 26:3).

Be the Sequoia Tree

WE CAN LEARN A GREAT deal about how to thrive in God's kingdom by studying details in nature. Take, for example, the giant sequoia tree, which can live up to three thousand years in even the harshest conditions. With their complex bark design, these towering treasures can survive wildfires and absorb the blow of fallen boulders. So how does one of the longest-living tree species stand up to these external challenges? You may be surprised to know that it is not through a hardened exterior but rather soft bundles of layered fibers.

Yes, the giant sequoia is one of the spongiest trees you will ever encounter. This provides a unique ability to withstand whatever may come. Not only does it endure catastrophe, but it also quickly returns to its original state largely unscathed. A sequoia's fortitude is so intriguing that researchers around the world are studying how to build earthquake-proof structures using a similar design. For men navigating the obstacles of our fallen world, there is a critical lesson in this. What does not bend will eventually break. Flexibility is not a point of weakness but robust strength.

Like the sequoia's bark that scientists now call a "three-dimensional network" of protection,[2] our God is also Three-in-One. With the help of the Father, Son, and Holy Spirit, we, too, can experience this same level of resiliency. This strength does not come from a hardened heart but from a soft, humble approach. There is power in bending our knees to pray.

Circumstances will not always go our way, and we will most certainly come against opposition. In studying the Word of God, we discover how the Lord's strength is often found by those who seek deeply and look beyond the obvious. And while the power of the Holy Spirit may not be outwardly visible, His presence resides within each one of us. Woven together by the threads of Christ's enduring love, we can withstand external challenges just as the sequoia tree.

KEY THOUGHT: Like the sequoia, God designed us to grow even through difficult seasons. With faith grounded in the Father, Son, and Holy Spirit, we draw ever closer to the glory He has prepared for us in Heaven.

ADDITIONAL READING:
- "A person standing alone can be attacked and defeated, but two can stand back-to-back and conquer. Three are even better, for a triple-braided cord is not easily broken" (Eccl. 4:12).

---

2   Georg Bold, Max Langer, Laura Börnert, and Thomas Speck, "The Protective Role of Bark and Bark Fibers of the Giant Sequoia (Sequoiadendron giganteum) during High-Energy Impacts," *International Journal of Molecular Sciences* 21, no. 9 (2020): 3355, https://doi.org/10.3390/ijms21093355.

- "For our present troubles are small and won't last very long. Yet they produce for us a glory that vastly outweighs them and will last forever" (2 Cor. 4:17).
- "That is why the Holy Spirit says, 'Today when you hear his voice, don't harden your hearts as Israel did when they rebelled, when they tested me in the wilderness'" (Heb. 3:7-8).
- "But we are citizens of heaven, where the Lord Jesus Christ lives. And we are eagerly waiting for him to return as our Savior" (Phil. 3:20).

Mental Health Matters

IN STUDYING GRAPHS THAT SHOW the decline of those practicing Christianity and the simultaneous increase in the use of antidepressants, many jump to conclude that the two are related. Some argue that there is more to it than meets the eye. These topics are anything but clear-cut, leaving more questions than answers.

The solution is certainly not a one-size-fits-all. In some cases, medication may indeed be necessary to correct a chemical imbalance. For others, engaging in prayer and making sense of one's existence with God is the answer. Why then can both of these paths not be followed concurrently? There seems to be a stigma around mental health medication in many Christian circles. And while it is true that doctors are often too quick to prescribe pills, medication has been proven effective in breaking vicious depressive cycles.

Wherever you may stand on mental health topics like medication and therapy, there is something on which we can all agree. The call to "man up" has proven to be deadly. To heap shame upon someone for using medications will only drive them further away from the Church. Regardless of your personal opinion on this, Jesus' followers should never alienate a hurt soul from connecting with God.

Scientists were given the gift of wisdom to create medication for people who need it. From this spiritual perspective, we find the need for compassion, upon which the lives of many depend, as does the revival we seek in the Church. Those who are hurting need Jesus desperately, and we must remove any barriers that may keep them away.

KEY THOUGHT: Jesus came to bridge the gap between us and God. Do not impede on His plan by passing judgment on those who are seeking additional help. Many lives are at stake, as is the health of the Church at large.

ADDITIONAL READING:

- "Going over to him, the Samaritan soothed his wounds with olive oil and wine and bandaged them. Then he put the man on his own donkey and took him to an inn, where he took care of him" (Luke 10:34).
- "All praise to God, the Father of our Lord Jesus Christ. God is our merciful Father and the source of all comfort. He comforts us in all our troubles so that we can comfort others. When they are troubled, we will be able to give them the same comfort God has given us" (2 Cor. 1:3-4).
- "So let's stop condemning each other. Decide instead to live in such a way that you will not cause another believer to stumble and fall" (Rom. 14:13).
- "He heals the brokenhearted and bandages their wounds" (Psalm 147:3).

Scars That Go Unseen

STUDIES SHOW THAT AMERICAN MEN are three to four times as likely to commit suicide than women. This alarming inclination does not stop at the borders of the United States. Male suicide has become a global epidemic with far-reaching consequences. While the circumstances behind each loss of life vary, there is a clear common denominator. Men are suffering in silence, and more has to be done to turn around this devastating trend.

The biggest obstacle to overcome may indeed be our pride. Christian men want to lead their families, build careers, get involved in their children's lives, be loving husbands, and also grow their relationship with Jesus. This is a tall order for even the most well-intentioned among us. Yet despite the challenging nature of these goals, we are notoriously resistant to asking for help. We want to be seen as powerful and capable of handling any situation.

Depression, anxiety, and other mental health conditions thrive in places of solitude. Unlike broken bones and other physical wounds, the struggles of heart, mind, and soul often go unseen. This does not mean they are any less serious. When we are left to our own devices, we can wreak havoc on our lives and those we love.

While the inward scars may not be visible, Jesus knows all too well the pain they bring about. He walked this earth just as we do today and suffered unthinkable emotional distress. Staring down imminent death, He sweated drops of blood. Perhaps the imagery of this moment evokes feelings to which you can relate. The astonishing thing is that He endured this so that our sins would not keep us from God. Jesus understood the pain of being a man in this world and sacrificed Himself so that we would not have to endure it alone.

You may not have friends to turn to or people you can trust, but you are most certainly not alone. God has moved heaven and earth for the opportunity to keep you from harm. Let the truth of His love fill the places of darkness. Those scars, once hidden, will become the new starting line for your testimony with Jesus by your side.

Key Thought: The chains of depression may not be visible but can bring tragic consequences if left unaddressed. Jesus can ease your suffering and heal the wounds caused by these internal battles. When we pray for Him to move in these areas, our struggles become a position of power.

Additional Reading:
- "He prayed more fervently, and he was in such agony of spirit that his sweat fell to the ground like great drops of blood" (Luke 22:44).
- "'He will wipe every tear from their eyes, and there will be no more death or sorrow or crying or pain. All these things are gone forever'" (Rev. 21:4).

- "Though I am surrounded by troubles, you will protect me from the anger of my enemies. You reach out your hand, and the power of your right hand saves me" (Psalm 138:7).
- "I pray that God, the source of hope, will fill you completely with joy and peace because you trust in him. Then you will overflow with confident hope through the power of the Holy Spirit" (Rom. 15:13).

11

THE GOSPEL OF PEACE

READING THE BIBLE FREQUENTLY CAN heal parts of you that were once considered beyond repair. The verses you highlight will leave a visible trail of evidence across the pages. This is not merely an indication of what you have memorized but what has transformed you. In a world that tends to attack what it does not understand, this Holy Book is a form of self-defense. Let the words become imprinted upon your heart like letters chiseled into ancient tablets.

You have probably heard it said that God is the same today as He was yesterday and will be tomorrow (Heb. 13:8). The same is true with His Word. The Scripture has not been altered, but the person reading it will indeed change. This, of course, affects the world around you, especially those you hold closest. Over time, this ripple effect gathers strength and grows into transformative waves. Things that once seemed out of reach are ushered in with a new tide. Meanwhile, the old is swept out to sea and vanishes in the healing waters of God's vast love.

The Living Word is the full armor of God, and without it, there is little to protect us from the challenges we face. Unlike our other material possessions, the Bible brings us closer to Jesus each time we use it. It anchors our feet and grounds us in love so we can stand tall. Earthly distractions are put in their right place and separated like chaff from the wheat. We are then left with open hands, ready to accept the sustenance of God's Word. It is in this willingness to hear from Him that we unpack the peace within.

The abstractions of religion are wiped away by the blood of Jesus. The pages of Scripture detail not only Who God is but also what He has done to draw us near to Him. Only, this story does not end with the main character's death. Jesus' sacrifice was made for each of us to have a new beginning with God at the helm. Write the next chapter of your life with Him, and you will experience the glory only He can provide.

Key Thought: Think of the Bible as more than just a physical book. It is an answer to your prayers. It is God revealing Himself to you in a tangible way.

Additional Reading:
- "For shoes, put on the peace that comes from the Good News so that you will be fully prepared" (Eph. 6:15).
- "Study this Book of Instruction continually. Meditate on it day and night so you will be sure to obey everything written in it. Only then will you prosper and succeed in all you do" (Josh. 1:8).
- "For you have been born again, but not to a life that will quickly end. Your new life will last forever because it comes from the eternal, living word of God" (1 Peter 1:23).
- "And I am certain that God, who began the good work within you, will continue his work until it is finally finished on the day when Christ Jesus returns" (Phil. 1:6).

12
What Death Teaches Us About Life

DURING A RECENT MOVE, I found my old yearbook dating back to elementary school. I was ten at the time, but somehow, this little book survived thirty-plus years. Most of the entries offer simple phrases like "Have a great summer" or "Good luck next year." There is one particular page, however, with profound significance. It was written by my now-late father with his usual brand of philosophical insight. At the time, the depth of his message was lost on me. Yet all these years later, it feels more relevant than ever: "Success means never giving up. Love always, Dad."

Before he died at fifty-seven from melanoma, I gently held his hand and let the scene wash over me. Even with morphine patches, he would wince in pain with tumors protruding from his skeletal arms. He had been through several rounds of chemotherapy, radiation, and many major operations; but it was simply too late.

"I have done a lot of fighting," he managed to whisper.

I felt my heart break into pieces.

The next day, when I went back to the hospice room, he was still alive but no longer alert. He appeared to be hanging on, despite the intolerable pain. His body may have been failing, but his will to take care of his family was still strong.

"Dad," I said, "it is okay to let go. You have raised us all well, and we are capable of looking after ourselves and each other. We will be all right. You do not have to fight any longer. You are not giving up but going home."

He was motionless, but I truly believed he was capable of hearing my words at a deeper level. I taped a picture I had taken of a daffodil to one of the machines by his bed. I did not know it at the time, but this flower is said to be a symbol of rebirth and new beginnings.

The next time I saw my dad, his soul had departed. He was a man of lifelong faith, and I was comforted by the thought of him being with Jesus in Heaven. The room was eerily silent, and I saw firsthand how it is not someone's physical body we connect with but what is inside. Equally profound was the knowledge that death is not the end but a new chapter spent even closer with God.

It was this loss that helped me understand just how fleeting life is and how we need to make the most of our time on earth. Ironically, it was this painful experience that helped me get through future hardships as well, which involve never giving up and holding on even when hope is lost. It means continuing to give it your best shot until God decides it is your time to go back home and shine for all of eternity.

KEY THOUGHT: Losing a parent is painful, but when viewed from a spiritual perspective, death can teach us how to live.

Additional Reading:

- "So we are always confident, even though we know that as long as we live in these bodies we are not at home with the Lord. For we live by believing and not by seeing. Yes, we are fully confident, and we would rather be away from these earthly bodies, for then we will be at home with the Lord (2 Cor. 5:6-8).
- "But as for you, be strong and courageous, for your work will be rewarded" (2 Chron. 15:7).
- "Then, when our dying bodies have been transformed into bodies that will never die, this Scripture will be fulfilled: 'Death is swallowed up in victory'" (1 Cor. 15:54).
- "You will show me the way of life, granting me the joy of your presence and the pleasures of living with you forever" (Psalm 16:11).

13

SEEKING EXTRA HELP

THE CONCEPT OF PAYING A therapist to unpack your innermost thoughts can feel a bit strange. Pairing a soul-bearing act with a financial transaction can sow doubt. Questions like "Do they care about me, or is this all about the money?" come to mind. Yet this skepticism is flawed by one critical omission. A good counselor is not only just meant to listen but also to provide tools that uncover clarity and perspective.

To further complicate matters, many of us wrestle with shame over our need for additional support. We wonder why our relationship with God is not proving effective enough. Jesus is, after all, referred to as a "Wonderful Counselor" (Isa. 9:6) in the Bible. In seeking more help, though, it is not Him we are looking to change but us. Sometimes, new skills are necessary to make space for God to work. When you think of it this way, therapeutic talk sessions are well worth the cost.

Men, in particular, can be hesitant to take this crucial step for fear they will be seen as weak. This could not be further from the truth, though. Asking for assistance is a mark of tremendous courage. Taking charge of your mental health should be applauded. A good place to start is by talking with your pastor. Ask if they can recommend a therapist who is also a Christian. Chances are, you will not be the first (or last) person to inquire. When you approach it this way, you are not sidestepping God but including Him in the process.

KEY THOUGHT: If the path God created for you is obstructed by a troubled mind, a Christian counselor can offer the proper tools to clear the way for God's glory. By asking for help, you will overcome the negative trappings of pride.

ADDITIONAL READING:

- "Plans go wrong for lack of advice; many advisers bring success" (Prov. 15:22).
- "So humble yourselves under the mighty power of God, and at the right time he will lift you up in honor" (1 Peter 5:6).
- "As my life was slipping away, I remembered the Lord. And my earnest prayer went out to you in your holy Temple" (Jonah 2:7).
- "Fools think their own way is right, but the wise listen to others" (Prov. 12:15).

The Architect of Your Life

THE PLANS PREPARED BY AN architect are much like our desire to grow into a better person. On paper, the ideas are well-developed, but action is needed to create something tangible. For most dwellings, this starts by laying down a strong foundation. And while this structural part of the house will not add to its visual curb appeal, it is an essential step in the building process.

Our faith in God is quite similar. To leap from a mere desire to actual change starts with the foundation. Self-discipline is helpful, but our power can only take us so far. Eventually, storms come, and with them, we weaken and falter.

Can you imagine trying to hold up heavy beams of timber while gale-force winds howl through a structure? That is essentially the picture of a man without God as the Bedrock of his life. As men, we often mistake the need for help as a sign of weakness. Yet Jesus teaches us that it is a place of strength.

Take heart if you are currently at a point of desperation resulting from trials in your own life. Rock bottom may be painful, but it positions you perfectly to rebuild with God as your base Support. God promises that He alone is our Shelter, no matter how great the challenge.

Are you willing to surrender your old way of life to make space for the person you want to be? Turn your plans over to God, and the new you will begin to take shape.

Key Thought: During moments of difficulty, what strengths and weaknesses are revealed about your character? Choosing God as the Foundation of your life allows Him to build the person you were designed to be.

Additional Reading:

- "'But anyone who hears and doesn't obey is like a person who builds a house right on the ground, without a foundation. When the floods sweep down against that house, it will collapse into a heap of ruins'" (Luke 6:49).
- "God is our refuge and strength, always ready to help in times of trouble" (Psalm 46:1).
- "Yet God has made everything beautiful for its own time. He has planted eternity in the human heart, but even so, people cannot see the whole scope of God's work from beginning to end" (Eccl. 3:11).
- "This means that anyone who belongs to Christ has become a new person. The old life is gone; a new life has begun" (2 Cor. 5:17).

15

The Colorful Lens of Jesus

WHEN WE FOLLOW JESUS, OUR problems do not magically disappear. However, the lens through which we view the world does change. For some, this shift in perspective may not be readily apparent. Those who are new to Christianity sometimes comment that they still feel the same. What they are not yet recognizing is the way God is working within their hearts. Like a painter adding color to a blank canvas, God is transforming our souls one brushstroke at a time.

A dazzling example of this is the rare but brilliant lunar rainbow. A moonbow, as it is sometimes called, is a natural phenomenon that occurs under the light of a full moon. It is typically found in the mist created at the base of a waterfall. To the human eye, the bow appears to be largely monochromatic. In the faint evening light, our visual receptors simply are not stimulated enough to recognize the various hues. Yet if you set up a camera and lens to photograph this same scene, a vibrant display of bold colors is shown to be ever-present.

In our own fast-paced lives, it is easy to become so immersed in day-to-day activities that we miss the miraculous things God is doing right in front of us. In stepping back and looking at the big picture, we can fully grasp His faithfulness. Like the photographer who will eventually see the colorful moonbow on the camera's LCD screen, you will eventually see the wonderful thing Jesus is developing in you.

Prayer is an opportune way to connect directly with our Creator. Ask Him to reveal His purpose in your own life. Perhaps it will be your newfound perspective that can be used to reveal God's glory to those who do not yet know Him.

KEY THOUGHT: One can find many reasons to be skeptical, but it only widens the gap between you and God. Trusting what we cannot see is made possible by intentionally choosing to do so. Commit to put your faith in Jesus, even when His ways go beyond your earthly understanding.

ADDITIONAL READING:
- "The heavens proclaim the glory of God. The skies display his craftsmanship. Day after day they continue to speak; night after night they make him known" (Psalm 19:1-2).
- "And I will give you a new heart, and I will put a new spirit in you. I will take out your stony, stubborn heart and give you a tender, responsive heart" (Ezek. 36:26).
- "Faith shows the reality of what we hope for; it is the evidence of things we cannot see" (Heb. 11:1).
- "Only fools say in their hearts, 'There is no God.' They are corrupt, and their actions are evil; not one of them does good" (Psalm 14:1).

The Best Way to Hear God's Voice

HOW DO YOU CHOOSE TO digest new content? Today, there are more ways than ever before to absorb information, including audiobooks, written copy, videos, podcasts, and even image-driven memes. There is a method to suit just about every learning style and attention span. Some of us are more visual, while others prefer to listen or write things down. Understanding your ideal process can be helpful to consistently tune in to what God is speaking into your life.

God's primary way of communicating with us today is through His Word. If you are still hungry to hear more from the Lord, think about additional ways to supplement your learning. Our Creator knows the optimal ways to reach you. If studying artwork or listening to music helps bring further clarity to a biblical principle, the concepts may resonate in a new way. There is no definitively right method, despite what some people may tell you. God has taken extraordinary steps to remove any barriers that may keep us from Him.

Even the Bible can be approached through a variety of delivery methods. You can choose to listen to it or explore different written translations that may read more clearly. To deepen your understanding, add a few devotionals or an online sermon about the same concept. You can also use the concordance in the back of the Bible to locate specific topics.

You may find that highlighting favorite passages also creates a deeper connection to the living Word. Whether you are reading on a phone, tablet, or traditionally printed Bible, remember that God's Word is living and active (Heb. 4:12), and He is waiting to connect with you in a profound way.

KEY THOUGHT: To supercharge your Bible reading and take your faith to the next level, seek to expand your knowledge of God's Word through a variety of additional resources.

ADDITIONAL READING:

- "For the word of God is alive and powerful. It is sharper than the sharpest two-edged sword, cutting between soul and spirit, between joint and marrow. It exposes our innermost thoughts and desires" (Heb. 4:12).
- "Let me ask you this one question: Did you receive the Holy Spirit by obeying the law of Moses? Of course not! You received the Spirit because you believed the message you heard about Christ" (Gal. 3:2).
- "For this good news—that God has prepared this rest—has been announced to us just as it was to them. But it did them no good because they didn't share the faith of those who listened to God" (Heb. 4:2).

- "I pray that your hearts will be flooded with light so that you can understand the confident hope he has given to those he called—his holy people who are his rich and glorious inheritance" (Eph. 1:18).

Waiting on God to Deliver

EVERY PART OF OUR LIVES seems centered around instant gratification these days. We expect our online orders to arrive the very next day. Full seasons of shows are completed over a weekend of binge-watching. Even pizza deliveries have a tracker with a countdown to completion. You could argue that these are all modern conveniences, and in truth, they are. Yet the trade-off for this on-demand mentality is the erosion of our patience.

The tension, of course, is that God does not work in this fashion. Do not get me wrong—He is moving in everything we do, but it is in His time, not ours. This can be a hard transition for a modern society that has grown accustomed to having immediate access to everything. The difference is that God takes our prayers and uses them to build trust and change lives for the greater good. This will not always coincide with our scheduling needs.

When we are facing difficult trials, this waiting period is simply too much for many of us to bear. Whether we require healing, financial relief, mental peace, or some other urgent remedy, no one likes being in limbo for longer than necessary. The problem is that in trying to fast-forward through the waiting period, we are missing an opportunity to let God transform us on a deeper level. It is in the space in between our prayer and ultimate resolution that God does some of His best work.

If every issue were resolved the moment we said amen, would it make us better in the long run? Chances are we would become more impatient and lack the character to weather challenges of any kind. Worst of all, our relationship with Jesus would be likened to yet another app from which to order our earthly desires. God's love for us is infinitely deeper than that. He wants us to stay in frequent communication with Him, and this involves a persistent practice of patient prayer.

KEY THOUGHT: The help we so desperately seek may come in a different time frame than we had hoped, but God's response will be far greater than our initial request.

ADDITIONAL READING:

- "The Lord is good to those who depend on him, to those who search for him. So it is good to wait quietly for salvation from the Lord" (Lam. 3:25-26).
- "'My thoughts are nothing like your thoughts,' says the Lord. 'And my ways are far beyond anything you could imagine'" (Isa. 55:8).
- "Devote yourselves to prayer with an alert mind and a thankful heart" (Col. 4:2).
- "Now all glory to God, who is able, through his mighty power at work within us, to accomplish infinitely more than we might ask or think" (Eph. 3:20).

Bible Before Breaking News

WHEN YOU WAKE UP IN the morning, what is the first thing you look at? If it is the news or social media, you are inadvertently setting a pessimistic tone for the rest of the day. In fact, a recent study revealed that 90 percent of stories reported by the media are negative. And while our pocket-sized devices are certainly amazing, it is how we use them that ultimately leverages their power. You can navigate to the fear and anxiety of breaking news or the love and hope of the Bible. It is all right there at your fingertips.

Some say the human brain is predisposed to negative bias. Scientists have provided data to support this claim. If this is indeed accurate, we need to counter it with overwhelming positivity. Forging new pathways takes deliberate and consistent effort. One effective way is to open the Bible app before reading any news or social media posts. It is here in God's Word that you can determine what He has in store for you.

This does not mean you are turning a blind eye to the struggles of the world or choosing ignorance. The sensationalized headlines will still be there when you are done. The difference is that you will have the proper frame of mind to put them into perspective. This will carry over into your various interactions throughout the day. Rather than echoing darkness, you will be a reflection of God's love.

Key Thought: Technology may keep us plugged into worldly events, but this can take our focus away from Heavenly matters that have eternal impact. Create a new morning routine that prioritizes time in the Word over any other content. The benefits will shape not only your life but also that of those around you as well.

Additional Reading:
- "My child, pay attention to what I say. Listen carefully to my words. Don't lose sight of them. Let them penetrate deep into your heart, for they bring life to those who find them, and healing to their whole body" (Prov. 4:20-22).
- "'But the word of the Lord remains forever.' And that word is the Good News that was preached to you" (1 Peter 1:25).
- "Your word is a lamp to guide my feet and a light for my path" (Psalm 119:105).
- "Every word of God proves true. He is a shield to all who come to him for protection" (Prov. 30:5).

19
GOD IN THE UNEXPECTED

THE MOVIES, MUSIC, AND BOOKS you enjoy do not require a Christian label to unpack God's glory profoundly. He is found in all things, even when it is the last place you would think to look. The fact is, modern entertainment often pulls from biblical themes without attributing it as such. For those looking through a spiritual lens, there is a wealth of wisdom to extract.

Take, for example, the rock band U2. They are one of the most well-known music acts in the world. If you listen closely, you will hear the name of Jesus or other biblical references in nearly every song. Still, the band does not categorize their work as "worship music." You can find similar examples with many influential books and films as well. Here again, we see how God's vast reach cannot be contained by manmade categories and genres.

If God is at the center of all things in your life, you will recognize His presence even in things that may seem unorthodox at first. Of course, a certain level of discernment is wise, especially with children's entertainment. Still, keeping an open mind may indeed reveal God's Divine influence in more places than He is given credit for.

Fans of fiction books often cite C.S. Lewis's *The Lion, the Witch, and the Wardrobe* as the preeminent work in his collection. What many do not initially recognize are the metaphors woven throughout to express the victory found in Jesus' death. Yes, God can even be found in Narnia. And while some fault Lewis for what they call religious propaganda, his stories have made challenging spiritual topics more accessible for countless young readers.

God knows that not everyone is actively seeking Him at all times. Yet there is no mountain high enough to keep Him from pursuing His children. Even when we tune Him out, He comes in unexpected ways. Though you will not find His name in the credits of these projects, you can rest assured He played a major role in bringing them to life.

KEY THOUGHT: Jesus' love cannot be contained in a curated list of items meant solely for Christians. Just because the packaging is not faith-based, that does not mean God is not in it.

ADDITIONAL READING:
- "And later Isaiah spoke boldly for God, saying, 'I was found by people who were not looking for me. I showed myself to those who were not asking for me'" (Rom. 10:20).
- "'Can you solve the mysteries of God? Can you discover everything about the Almighty?'" (Job 11:7).
- "Then he said, 'Don't be afraid, Daniel. Since the first day you began to pray for understanding and to humble yourself before your God, your request has been heard in heaven. I have come in answer to your prayer'" (Dan. 10:12).
- "For whoever finds me finds life and receives favor from the Lord" (Prov. 8:35).

20
Accessing God's Prayer Support (GPS)

THE POTENTIAL FOR BREAKDOWNS IS part of the deal when you own a vehicle. Perhaps you left the headlights on, and the battery died; or your tire was punctured, causing it to go flat. In more serious cases, a major repair may be required. Regardless of the cause, it is extremely helpful to have someone to call on should you find yourself stuck on the side of the road. The problem is that our friends and family are not always available to help. This is not a criticism but merely a circumstance of our modern, hectic lives. As a result, we need to seek assistance from another source, such as a roadside service.

This same reality often plays out in other areas of our lives. One minute, we are riding high with abundant joy, only to come crashing down from an unexpected event. The support network of family and friends may be well-intentioned, but they cannot possibly understand the nuances of our every struggle. They may even reside in a different time zone and are sound asleep in another part of the world.

In God, we have full access to an omnipresent and compassionate Lord. Regardless of your location or time of day, He is always there in your moment of need. You do not need an app, membership, or even battery life to call. Jesus' sacrifice on the cross destroyed any barriers that kept us from God.

The Lord has an impeccable track record for those who pray. No issue is too trivial or dire for Him to lend a hand. He has the power to take our brokenness and use it to fuel our next move. There is no need to be eloquent in your conversations with God, but rather be open and honest. I have even heard about people who never say amen, as they want to stay in contact with Jesus all day, every day. This is the level of detailed involvement God wants with us. Do you want to risk proceeding without GPS and roadside assistance or allow Him to guide you to safety?

KEY THOUGHT: Jesus meets us right where we are, even when we find ourselves most distant. If you have been navigating through life without Him, there is no time like the present to surrender the keys and let Him jumpstart your heart.

ADDITIONAL READING:
- "Are any of you suffering hardships? You should pray. Are any of you happy? You should sing praises" (James 5:13).
- "I prayed to the Lord, and he answered me. He freed me from all my fears" (Psalm 34:4).
- "Search for the Lord and for his strength; continually seek him" (1 Chron. 16:11).
- "'For the Lord your God is living among you. He is a mighty savior. He will take delight in you with gladness. With his love, he will calm all your fears. He will rejoice over you with joyful songs'" (Zeph. 3:17).

21
First Aid Faith

IN TALKING WITH OTHER CHRISTIAN men, a common pattern is evident in many of our walks with God. It starts when struggles arise and our prayer life picks up with renewed vigor. During these periods, we can be seen at church with hands raised in worship. At home, we read new devotionals, talk with God, and praise His faithfulness as our prayers are answered. Yet when the turbulence eventually calms, our daily communication with Jesus often grinds to a halt. This routine is something with which I am certainly well-acquainted. I would best describe it as a first-aid type of faith. We lean on God through the valley and turn away on the mountaintop.

Why do we do this to ourselves and, more importantly, to God? The answer may be found in our prideful tendencies. "I have got this," we say while working through situations in our own strength. And in truth, things may feel very much under control. In a twist of irony, we are so abundantly blessed that it is easy to lose sight of God's involvement. This causes friction as our focus wanes from seeking His will to relying on ours.

To form a new, more consistent relationship with God, it is necessary to give Him the glory in each victory. When you reach a place of personal satisfaction, know that it was not through your craftsmanship but His. The Lord rains down mercy and grace, not because of our accomplishments but in order to reveal His neverending love for us. Without acknowledging this, we are taking credit for being the author of our own lives. By humbly praising the triumphs and trusting through the trials, we become a bigger part of His amazing story.

KEY THOUGHT: Grow closer to God by putting Him first in all seasons of your life. In times of celebration, give Him the glory for helping to achieve your accomplishments. When inevitable periods of darkness gather, use them as an opportunity to shine even brighter.

ADDITIONAL READING:

- "Search for the Lord and for his strength; continually seek him" (Psalm 105:4).
- "God saved you by his grace when you believed. And you can't take credit for this; it is a gift from God" (Eph. 2:8).
- "Their loyalty is divided between God and the world, and they are unstable in everything they do" (James 1:8).
- "Yours, O Lord, is the greatness, the power, the glory, the victory, and the majesty. Everything in the heavens and on earth is yours, O Lord, and this is your kingdom. We adore you as the one who is over all things" (1 Chron. 29:11).

22

Lifting the Bible

IS THE BIBLE TRULY ONE of the most frequently stolen books in the world? Well, according to bookstores and libraries, this is indeed accurate.[3] This leads to the next obvious question: why? One theory is that a vast number of people recognize their need for God's help but are too embarrassed to acknowledge it with a purchase. It is sort of like buying lice treatment from a pharmacy. You have an issue that needs to be addressed but cringe at the thought of being exposed when you go to the checkout.[4]

Thankfully, it is this type of shame that Jesus turns around throughout the Scriptures. Of course, shoplifting a Bible is not the right way of finding the truth, but it certainly may be symbolic of the transformative power of God's Word. Whatever situation you may be struggling with, there is wisdom to guide you through it. This itself confirms that we are not alone in our woes. We have all been immersed in trials we would rather not endure. Seeking help from the Lord, therefore, puts us in exceptional company.

---

3   Orion, "Stealing knowledge: Which are the most frequently stolen books from libraries?," The Brain Maze, September 2, 2019, https://thebrainmaze.com/stealing-knowledge-what-are-the-most-frequently-stolen-books-from-libraries.
4   Graemme Marshall, "The Bible: The World's Most Shoplifted Book?," Church of God, February 24, 2014, https://lifehopeandtruth.com/prophecy/blog/the-bible-the-worlds-most-shoplifted-book.

Before His crucifixion, Jesus asked God three times for His trial to pass. Of course, He willingly fulfilled God's plan but not before agonizing over it. This is just one of the countless examples of the plight of man and the very real pain of the human condition.

In this, we see that there is no reason to hide your need for God. Sure, some will criticize and may even call you crazy or weak. Others may tell you it is a manmade crutch used to control people. Ironically, these very statements are an attempt to assert authority over your spiritual beliefs. Considering that these comments can come from parents and others we respect, it is no wonder the Bible is stolen so often.

Like all great books, the Bible is full of plot twists. So, here is a litmus test to clarify who has your best interests at heart. God will forgive you for stealing a Bible, but will those who condemn your decision to read it offer you the same grace?

KEY THOUGHT: Let God's Word be your hiding place, rather than a title to smuggle under wraps.

ADDITIONAL READING:
- "Many will follow their evil teaching and shameful immorality. And because of these teachers, the way of truth will be slandered" (2 Peter 2:2).
- "But the Lord will redeem those who serve him. No one who takes refuge in him will be condemned" (Psalm 34:22).
- "'There is no judgment against anyone who believes in him. But anyone who does not believe in him has already

been judged for not believing in God's one and only Son'" (John 3:18).
- "But God showed his great love for us by sending Christ to die for us while we were still sinners" (Rom. 5:8).

23

THE ULTIMATE
HOW-TO GOD

IN MY TOWN, THERE IS a small yellow signpost to let visitors know which road leads to the church. Before becoming a member of my congregation, I jogged past this street sign dozens of times without ever noticing. It was during a particularly challenging season in my life, and long-distance running had become my form of church. The irony, of course, is that I was running to fill the void created by turning from God. In truth, I did become physically stronger, but my mind and soul were anything but healthy.

Today, we have scores of men's magazines and websites that celebrate a do-it-yourself spirit. Watch enough instructional videos and read the right tutorials, and you can teach yourself just about anything. Yet with this self-reliant mindset, how many signs pointing to God go unnoticed? You may be able to stop the pipe from leaking with plumber's tape, but if the root problem is not resolved, it will eventually burst with destructive consequences.

God has already provided the ultimate how-to guide, and His name is Jesus. While we take all the wrong turns, He is right there with us. Some of the roads we travel may even lead to dark and painful places. In looking at His promises in the Bible, though, you can see the trail of once-overlooked signs. The route has been carefully designed to lead us back to Him. It is now time to let Jesus take control of the wheel. The destination is eternal life, and He is the only Way to get there.

Key Thought: When you look back on your life's journey, it is clear to see how God used past struggles to create something even more beautiful than you imagined.

Additional Reading:

- "The Lord says, 'I will guide you along the best pathway for your life. I will advise you and watch over you'" (Psalm 32:8).
- "And I am convinced that nothing can ever separate us from God's love. Neither death nor life, neither angels nor demons, neither our fears for today nor our worries about tomorrow—not even the powers of hell can separate us from God's love" (Rom. 8:38).
- "He renews my strength. He guides me along right paths, bringing honor to his name" (Psalm 23:3).
- "Jesus told him, 'I am the way, the truth, and the life. No one can come to the Father except through me. If you had really known me, you would know who my Father is. From now on, you do know him and have seen him!'" (John 14:6-7).

24

WHAT BRINGS US TOGETHER?

TO UNDERSTAND WHAT BRINGS US together, we need to first consider what divides us. Borders, politics, and social debates are all obvious, but what about religion? It can sometimes appear that this is the most divisive topic of all. Even with all the bloodshed in past religious wars, heated tension among Christian denominations continues to this very day. Sometimes, it can take place within the same walls of a single church.

To underscore the urgent need for unity, the topic is mentioned throughout Scripture, from the Old to the New Testament. Meanwhile, just a cursory look at today's current events will reveal anything but harmony. A religious scholar is not necessary to point out just how badly we have missed the mark. As a result, the Church at large is missing a critical opportunity to effectively communicate God's love.

How then do we walk peacefully with those who may have different beliefs? A great starting point is found in the first two words of the Lord's Prayer: "Our Father" (Matt. 6:9). Pause and reflect on that for a moment. We are all God's children, regardless of our differences and however drastic they may be. By digging our heels into deeply entrenched positions, we are unraveling the Heavenly threads that bring us together. Those who follow Jesus are called to view things from a Kingdom perspective. We already know the enemy wants to divide and conquer. The real fight then is for unity rather than separation.

The common ground we all seek can only be found by walking together. If we want God's kingdom to be "on earth as it is in heaven" (Matt. 6:10), we must surrender to His will. We all benefit from trusting God with topics that are beyond our control. He uses every situation for good but sometimes does so in ways we cannot fully comprehend. Faith is placing our weapons down, coming together, and believing that God has it all worked out exactly as it should be. You may vehemently disagree with a group's position, but love is the only thing strong enough to bridge the divide.

KEY THOUGHT: It is our Father Who originally brought us together but did so by creating each of us with different thoughts and ideas. As heirs to God's kingdom, we must accept these differences as a necessary part of fulfilling His greater plan.

ADDITIONAL READING:
- "Can two people walk together without agreeing on the direction" (Amos 3:3).
- "Just as our bodies have many parts and each part has a special function, so it is with Christ's body. We are many parts of one body, and we all belong to each other" (Rom. 12:4-5).

- "I appeal to you, dear brothers and sisters, by the authority of our Lord Jesus Christ, to live in harmony with each other. Let there be no divisions in the church. Rather, be of one mind, united in thought and purpose" (1 Cor. 1:10).
- "For Christ himself has brought peace to us. He united Jews and Gentiles into one people when, in his own body on the cross, he broke down the wall of hostility that separated us" (Eph. 2:14).

25
I Will Pray for You

IF WE ARE NOT GENUINE in our prayer life, we risk these important words—"I will pray for you"—losing their meaning. We see it in politics all the time after any horrific event unfolds. Our social media feeds look like nothing more than a copy-and-paste campaign of *#thoughtsandprayers*. Yet if we are interested in bringing about change in our homes, churches, and communities, a more heartfelt approach is required.

I am not trying to get confrontational with you, but have you ever told someone you would pray for them, only to let it fall to the wayside? In full transparency, I most certainly have. Even with apps that remind us to pray, the notifications sometimes come through when we are busy with work or some other urgent task. So, how can we make sure nothing else slips through the cracks in moving forward?

It may be time to rethink your idea of prayer. There is no need for long, drawn-out sessions with exquisitely crafted language. It can be as simple as a page taped onto your closet door or in your journal. Give it a header like "I Ask in Faith" and hang a pen nearby for easy access. It only takes a few seconds to write, "Prayers for my wife's doctor appointment to show nothing serious and lead to healing and relief." If more details need to be added on subsequent days, just jot down the new request. "Please let the new medicine be the right solution with no negative side effects." Over a week, month, and year, you will have a visual roadmap to show how God has been moving in your life and in those for whom you have prayed.

Key Thought: Our prayer life is not meant to be an elaborate undertaking. In writing down short but frequent prayers, God's love can be seen between the lines.

Additional Reading:
- "Then the Lord said to me, 'Write my answer plainly on tablets, so that a runner can carry the correct message to others'" (Hab. 2:2).
- "And since we know he hears us when we make our requests, we also know that he will give us what we ask for" (1 John 5:15).
- "'When you pray, don't babble on and on as the Gentiles do. They think their prayers are answered merely by repeating their words again and again'" (Matt. 6:7).
- "But then I recall all you have done, O Lord; I remember your wonderful deeds of long ago. They are constantly in my thoughts. I cannot stop thinking about your mighty works" (Psalm 77:11-12).

26
The Logic of God Is Love

SIGNS OF A MENTALITY OF indebtedness are found throughout our society. If you owe the bank money, you are said to be burdened with liability. The transaction will be considered "forgiven" only when paid in full. We are even assigned credit scores that determine our fiscal worthiness. From a financial perspective, you are considered high-risk until proven otherwise. Some call this a necessary system of checks and balances. In fairness, they can be effective for keeping things in order when used properly. The problem, however, is when we view our relationship with God in the same way.

This could not be farther from the truth. Jesus loves us knowing full well all of our sins, shortcomings, and character flaws. You do not need to pay Him back or work to earn His affection. There is no reward system to buy your way into Heaven. Jesus came to make a way for those willing to follow.

The Bible tells of countless times Jesus sought to heal those on the outskirts of town. The marginalized, misunderstood, sick, poor, and crippled were all priorities, not problems. Look at the people with whom He was closest. They were certainly not religious scholars or elite members of society. Yet each one of His disciples was chosen to reveal the true nature of God's restorative love.

This logic is on full display in the story of the adulteress found in John 8:1-11. This woman had broken the law and was on the verge of being stoned to death. Not only did Jesus save her life, but in a beautiful show of mercy, He also did not condemn her for this sin. Here, the King of kings, with full authority to judge, chooses to set her free and encourages her to change her ways.

If you look closely at your own life, you will see a trail of God's mercy and grace, even when it was not earned. What a gift to know our Savior does not hold our past over our heads. Instead, our past is used as a way to bring us closer to Him through unfailing love.

Key Thought: When it seems the world is shutting doors around you, remain confident that God will lead you in a new and better direction.

Additional Reading:
- "Now repent of your sins and turn to God, so that your sins may be wiped away" (Acts 3:19).
- "Then Jesus stood up again and said to the woman, 'Where are your accusers? Didn't even one of them condemn you?' 'No, Lord,' she said. And Jesus said, 'Neither do I. Go and sin no more'" (John 8:10-11).
- "The Lord is good to everyone. He showers compassion on all his creation" (Psalm 145:9).
- "'I tell you the truth, those who listen to my message and believe in God who sent me have eternal life. They will never be condemned for their sins, but they have already passed from death into life'" (John 5:24).

27
Confronted by Jesus

HAVE YOU EVER ASKED JESUS to heal a broken relationship only to be told it is you who should apologize? Perhaps you shake your head and second-guess this directive. "Did God really ask me to do that, or was it just my imagination?" So, you continue to pray and are again confronted with the same instruction.

"Be the peacekeeper," He says, "and apologize for all the ways you have wronged them."

If you are anything like most men, admitting a fault to someone who also hurt you is a hard pill to swallow. You may even be tempted to simply ignore God's communication altogether—only, this is not the kind of message you can swipe left to delete. Left unchecked, bitterness will infiltrate every part of your being until there is no space remaining for happiness. A heart that feeds on resentment will soon be starved for love. As a result, we grow distant from God.

Acknowledging your shortcomings does not mean you agree with the offending person's actions. It does, however, extend grace in a way that honors Jesus' ultimate sacrifice for us. His selfless act covered all of our sins, including those we have yet to commit. This was not predicated on who was least guilty or if the other person admitted their part in it. Jesus calls us to love others, even those we consider enemies. When we apologize, it is a confession of our sins. In doing so, He promises that we, too, are forgiven.

KEY THOUGHT: We all want big change, but are we willing to take the steps that lead us there? Following Jesus requires us to lay down our pride and confess our wrongdoing. This does not make us weak but grows our character and relationship with God.

ADDITIONAL READING:
- "Some people make cutting remarks, but the words of the wise bring healing" (Prov. 12:18).
- "'So if you are presenting a sacrifice at the altar in the Temple and you suddenly remember that someone has something against you, leave your sacrifice there at the altar. Go and be reconciled to that person. Then come and offer your sacrifice to God'" (Matt. 5:23-24).
- "'But when you are praying, first forgive anyone you are holding a grudge against, so that your Father in heaven will forgive your sins, too'" (Mark 11:25).
- "If someone claims, 'I know God,' but doesn't obey God's commandments, that person is a liar and is not living in the truth. But those who obey God's word truly show how completely they love him. That is how we know we are living in him. Those who say they live in God should live their lives as Jesus did" (1 John 2:4-6).

28
Meant to Love

HAVING ENEMIES DOES NOT MAKE you a bad Christian. A quick look through the New Testament will reveal that Jesus had foes as well. It was, however, the revolutionary way He dealt with them that ultimately changed the world. The Bible provides a road map for handling our conflicts with His wisdom. While the directives are spelled out rather clearly in Scripture, following through with them is a tall order for even the most faithful followers of Jesus.

Phrases about loving our enemies, turning the other cheek, and refraining from retaliation are all challenging ideas on their own. Add to this a series of personal attacks, and it seems downright impossible to love your enemies. Working in our strength alone, we will fall short more often than not. When the heat is turned up and tempers flare, tenderness is usually the first thing to flee.

Have you ever been spit upon, insulted, mocked, wrongly accused, attacked spiritually, or emotionally and physically abused? Jesus endured all of this and then allowed Himself to be crucified. But while He was peaceful, Jesus' methods were anything but passive. His mind-blowing response is not one of retribution but rather of asking God to forgive His enemies. Could you or I be so bold and selfless?

To love those who persecute us is a supporting pillar of our faith. Do not allow vengeance to bring it tumbling down. After all, we are called to imitate Christ. And while it will not come easily at first, it can be done with His help. It involves replacing our disdain with compassion. Pray for a renewed heart, and the stranglehold of animosity will be released. It is with His grace that peace can flow through you like a river.

Key Thought: Loving people who come against us is perhaps the most challenging aspect of being a Christian. Reflect on the suffering Jesus willingly endured and seek His strength to sustain you.

Additional Reading:

- "Think of all the hostility he endured from sinful people; then you won't become weary and give up" (Heb. 12:3).
- "For God called you to do good, even if it means suffering, just as Christ suffered for you. He is your example, and you must follow in his steps" (1 Peter 2:21).
- "But I say, love your enemies! Pray for those who persecute you" (Matt. 5:44).
- "Jesus said, 'Father, forgive them, for they don't know what they are doing.' And the soldiers gambled for his clothes by throwing dice" (Luke 23:34).

When the Luster Fades

WE MUST WORK DILIGENTLY TO keep the flame burning bright in our marital relationships. This is typically easy to do during courtship as things are still new, mysterious, and exciting. Throughout a marriage, though, the luster can fade. This is not to say we do not still love our partner, but life throws a series of curveballs that require a thoughtful approach. Add the challenge of kids, money, health, and differences of opinion, and we can slowly drift apart. Soon we find ourselves immersed in the "for worse" portion of our vows and wondering if it will ever get better. Without changing course, we will become yet another divorce statistic.

In full disclosure, I am one of those men. I wrestled with shame after my divorce and considered giving up on love altogether. Yet after a long period of spiritual healing and self-reflection, God gave me another chance. This gift was to be cherished, and He provided biblical insight on how to best proceed. Here are the three main takeaways I found with His guidance.

Most importantly, God has to come first so you can be the best version of yourself for your spouse and your family. This can seem counterintuitive, as it involves spending time glorifying God rather than always focusing on your wife. The trade-off is that she will enjoy a spiritually grounded man who works to honor and love her for the foreseeable future. It is not about keeping score or being right but being the husband God called you to be. It means being "quick to listen . . . and slow to get angry" (James 1:19), not holding grudges, and humbling yourself to grow in areas that need improving. It is about serving your wife sacrificially and expecting nothing back in return. Some will argue that this just makes you a doormat. If done right, you will be a doormat but only in the best way possible. You want to be the welcome sign that lets her know she is home.

The next important step is to continue courting your wife long after saying "I do." Just as God relentlessly pursues us, we must do the same in our relationship. This is not just a single grand gesture but daily reminders that let her know how much you love her. It could be a note slipped under her dinner plate or a block of chocolate you sneak into her car while she is at work. Perhaps it is a candlelit dinner at home with a handwritten menu that names her as the guest of honor. You can order flowers "just because" or give her an unexpected back massage. None of this has to come with extravagant costs. Small but consistent acts of love make a bigger impact than even the most expensive piece of jewelry.

As followers of Jesus, we also need to pray for our wives. Rest your hand on her head at night and thank God for your bond. Ask Him to let nothing divide what He has brought together. Offer praise for all that is good and request help in any areas that may be challenging. All of this takes just a moment but will make for a lifetime of happiness.

KEY THOUGHT: Your spouse is a gift from God and needs to be loved in the same way Jesus cares for each of us. It will not always be easy, but there is no greater joy than sharing your life with the one with Whom He has blessed you.

ADDITIONAL READING:

- "Then the Lord God said, 'It is not good for the man to be alone. I will make a helper who is just right for him'" (Gen. 2:18).
- "You have captured my heart, my treasure, my bride. You hold it hostage with one glance of your eyes, with a single jewel of your necklace" (Song of Songs 4:9).
- "For husbands, this means love your wives, just as Christ loved the church. He gave up his life for her to make her holy and clean, washed by the cleansing of God's word. He did this to present her to himself as a glorious church without a spot or wrinkle or any other blemish. Instead, she will be holy and without fault. In the same way, husbands ought to love their wives as they love their own bodies. For a man who loves his wife actually shows love for himself" (Eph. 5:25-28).
- "'Since they are no longer two but one, let no one split apart what God has joined together'" (Matt. 19:6).

30
Putting the Context Back into Sex

SEX IS ONE OF THE fruits of a loving marriage. In the first book of the Bible, we find Adam and Eve naked and unashamed in a garden. God tells them to enjoy each other and multiply. While conceiving children is one of the reasons sex was created, it is not the whole story. If you continue reading through all sixty-six books of the Word, you will discover that making love is about so much more than procreating. It is a God-given way for a couple to delight in each other and enjoy their marital bond.

Many people are surprised to learn about the more intimate scenes depicted in the Bible. In the Song of Solomon, for example, we read passionate prose between a husband and wife who long for each other's touch. Some question why this was even included in Scripture. Yet every part of the Bible is inspired by God, so He certainly considers it an important topic. We are called to be generous with our spouses and have sex frequently. It is not just about the physical connection but becoming one flesh on a deeper spiritual level.

Many Christians shy away from this topic or even hide their desire to be intimate. This shame is not from God but rather stems from humans who have misinterpreted the Bible or taken it out of context. It is here that the waters are muddied and problems arise. It does not have to be this way. Sex is not framed as merely a suggestion in Scripture but as a need that should be embraced. It is a way to humble yourself before your spouse, be vulnerable, and connect in a deep way that was created by God.

As Christian men, we need to prioritize this act as more than just an afterthought. It means being intentional, setting aside time, and initiating lovemaking. Make a special playlist, light a candle, and enjoy the union that God has blessed you with. When you embrace your spouse, you become the type of loving husband the Bible calls you to be.

KEY THOUGHT: The Bible describes sex and romance as a necessary and healthy part of a marriage. Embrace your sexuality and honor your union often by sharing intimacy with your spouse.

ADDITIONAL READING:
- "Do not deprive each other of sexual relations, unless you both agree to refrain from sexual intimacy for a limited time so you can give yourselves more completely to prayer. Afterward, you should come together again so that Satan won't be able to tempt you because of your lack of self-control" (1 Cor. 7:5).
- "You are my private garden, my treasure, my bride, a secluded spring, a hidden fountain" (Song of Songs 4:12).

- "Oh, how beautiful you are! How pleasing, my love, how full of delights" (Song of Songs 7:6).
- "Let your wife be a fountain of blessing for you. Rejoice in the wife of your youth. She is a loving deer, a graceful doe. Let her breasts satisfy you always. May you always be captivated by her love" (Prov. 5:18-19).

31

DO IT WITHOUT GRIPING

TO BE "A MAN AFTER [Jesus'] own heart" (1 Sam. 13:14) requires that we serve others willingly. Responsibilities like grocery shopping, picking the kids up from practice, and cooking dinner may sound and be mundane; but they teach us how to walk in humility. As Christian men, we know this to be true and usually offer to help out where needed.

The problem, however, is the spirit in which it is sometimes done. If you are grumbling about missing the game while doing the dishes, it is hardly a selfless act of service.

How then do we accomplish this when life gets hectic and there are still needs to be addressed? The solution comes with a shift in perspective. Try changing your narrative from "I have to" to a more grateful approach like "I get to." It is a simple way to reexamine any undertaking that once seemed inconvenient. More importantly, it shows love, respect, and appreciation for those we are serving. The tension falls away when you reframe a task like this: "I get to prepare a nourishing meal for my wife and family whom I love so dearly."

When Jesus talks about the Golden Rule, He calls us to treat others with the same kindness we would like to receive. He knew it would not be effortless and suggests that most of us will fall short. Yet He provides a powerful illustration of why it is worth going the extra mile. The easy way leads to destruction, He says, while the hard way yields life (Matt. 7:13-14). This is the mindset of Christ, and following it is the best path to peace.

It is not about keeping score or going out of your way to get something in return. Jesus never said, "One hand washes the other." Instead, He washes the disciples' feet to make His point. It was a job typically reserved for servants, but here was the Son of Man doing it Himself. The King of kings was on His knees, not demanding to be served but humbling Himself before those He loved. Considering that most people wore sandals in those days, it was likely a messy process. This is a significant detail as it shows us how to proceed in our own lives. Roll up your sleeves, get your hands dirty, and serve others. In doing so, you will be fulfilling your part in the body of Christ.

KEY THOUGHT: It is with a servant's heart that we learn how to truly love. It may be a dirty job, but in growing more like Jesus, you will find your true reward.

ADDITIONAL READING:
- "Do everything without complaining and arguing" (Phil. 2:14).
- "He sat down, called the twelve disciples over to him, and said, 'Whoever wants to be first must take last place and be the servant of everyone else'" (Mark 9:35).

- "I have given you an example to follow. Do as I have done to you" (John 13:15).
- "'For even the Son of Man came not to be served but to serve others and to give his life as a ransom for many'" (Matt. 20:28).

Caught in the Act

IF YOU ASK TEN DIFFERENT dads about how they raise their kids, you will likely hear an equal number of parenting techniques. These typically range from a firm, no-nonsense approach to a more relaxed variety. With studies that detail the pros and cons of all these methods, it is challenging to settle on the best practice. Despite the differences, experts in this field do seem to agree on one prevailing concept. When it comes to kids, more is caught than taught.

This is certainly applicable when it comes to growing your children's convictions. Telling them that you believe in God is all well and good. Yet it is the examples you set while living out your faith that will make a more lasting impact. If they see Dad skip church on Sundays during football season, it sends a message that sports are more important than God. Likewise, if we are quick to anger and use heated language, guess who will do it next? During our children's formative years, it is ultimately our actions that will show them what it means to follow Jesus.

This can feel like a daunting task, especially if we feel unqualified to lead in this way. "I am far from perfect," we say. "How can I teach my kid about God?" It is this discomfort, though, that provides a powerful window of opportunity to develop your child's faith. You can say something like, "Daddy does not always get it right. I need help and forgiveness every day from Jesus to be the best version of myself. The truth is, we all need those things, even you and Mommy. Why do not we pray together to ask Him to work in all of our lives?"

Key Thought: Our little ones watch us more closely than we realize. Show them how you interact with God, and they will soon follow.

Additional Reading:
- "Now someone may argue, 'Some people have faith; others have good deeds.' But I say, 'How can you show me your faith if you don't have good deeds? I will show you my faith by my good deeds'" (James 2:18).
- "In the same way, let your good deeds shine out for all to see, so that everyone will praise your heavenly Father" (Matt. 5:16).
- "Seek the Kingdom of God above all else, and live righteously, and he will give you everything you need" (Matt. 6:33).
- "And you must commit yourselves wholeheartedly to these commands that I am giving you today. Repeat them again and again to your children. Talk about them when you are at home and when you are on the road, when you are going to bed and when you are getting up" (Deut. 6:6-7).

33

LET JESUS BE THE GOALIE

YOU LIKELY HAVE PEOPLE IN your life who are close to you but far from God. Maybe it is a child, a sibling, or a spouse. Naturally, you want what is best for them and are concerned for the well-being of their soul. Despite these good intentions, they may still feel that Jesus is not the answer. No matter how many miraculous ways God reveals Himself, they are not receiving the message. As Christians, we need to understand that they may not want to see it.

This is a hard pill to swallow when it is someone you love deeply. It can be frustrating to watch them succumb to ongoing spiritual attacks and still shut God out. If we are not careful, we can view their lack of faith as our fault. This is dangerous, though, as the more we push, the further away they get. In the worst instances, it can divide a relationship altogether. This is not what Jesus envisioned when He called the disciples to be fishers of men.

How then do we lead our families spiritually? It is not all that different from being part of a soccer team. Just as there are forwards, midfielders, and defenders, we all have a unique role to play. Our job is to reflect God's light through our actions. If someone slips through the cracks like a soccer ball does through team formation, who better to be the Goalie than Jesus? As the Shepherd of men, He has promised to search high and low to save all who are lost.

Pray for the Holy Spirit to tend the seeds you have planted; and one day, the faith of your loved one will bloom. Admittedly, it can be disheartening to continue praying for someone who does not realize they need to be saved. It may even feel like you are passing the buck to let God do the heavy lifting. When it comes to spiritual matters, the battle is the Lord's alone.

KEY THOUGHT: When it seems all hope is lost, maintain faith in Jesus' promise to protect and save every last one of His flock.

ADDITIONAL READING:
- "On that day the Lord their God will rescue his people, just as a shepherd rescues his sheep. They will sparkle in his land like jewels in a crown" (Zech. 9:16).
- "I have other sheep, too, that are not in this sheepfold. I must bring them also. They will listen to my voice, and there will be one flock with one shepherd" (John 10:16).
- "And because we are his children, God has sent the Spirit of his Son into our hearts, prompting us to call out, 'Abba, Father.' Now you are no longer a slave but God's own child. And since you are his child, God has made you his heir" (Gal. 4:6-7).
- "'And everyone assembled here will know that the Lord rescues his people, but not with sword and spear. This is the Lord's battle, and he will give you to us!'" (1 Sam. 17:47).

Family Is Not a Weakness

FINDING A HEALTHY WORK/LIFE BALANCE is essential if you are to maintain the bandwidth needed to accomplish God's purpose. Some companies are more concerned with their cash flow than the well-being of those who help them earn it. While this is certainly not ideal, it makes sense from a business perspective. There is always pressure from either a CEO, CFO, or various board members to continually improve the bottom line. This is what they were trained and hired to do.

What is missing from their spreadsheets is a column for employee satisfaction. And since it is not a PowerPoint slide on their key performance indicators, it needs to be part of ours. It is our responsibility alone to set boundaries around our job and family time. Contrary to what some may believe, this is anything but selfish. Simply put, a happy employee is far more productive than one who feels taken advantage of.

I once declined a job offer for a great role that had really poor hours. The *minimum* requirements were from 7:00 a.m. to 5:00 p.m., Monday to Friday. Doing the math, that is a fifty-hour work week with little time for anything else. Rather than simply saying no, I explained that as a Christian family man, my employer must have a similar ethos to mine. I am eager to work hard, but there needs to be a counterbalance with the other parts of my life.

Considering I had nothing to lose and everything to gain, I emailed a short list of requests to the managing director. I asked for a more flexible schedule with hours from 9:00 a.m. to 4:00 p.m. Then I stated that the position should be remote, meaning I work from home 100 percent of the time. I also requested that the company's contribution to my retirement fund be increased and that they pay for any training or software that could further develop my job-related skills. After clicking "send," I figured I would never hear anything back.

Yet as God has repeatedly demonstrated throughout my life, He provides in abundance. Not only did the company agree to all the points presented but three months later they also increased my salary by 5 percent and an additional 30 percent on my one-year employment anniversary. I have been able to help the company gain market share while also maintaining time for God, myself, and my family.

KEY THOUGHT: If we are afraid to be different and stand out from the rest, will we ever be seen for who we truly are? God measures success in the way we love Him and those around us, not by our ability to hit revenue goals.

ADDITIONAL READING:
- "'No one can serve two masters. For you will hate one and love the other; you will be devoted to one and despise the

other. You cannot serve God and be enslaved to money'" (Matt. 6:24).
- "Children are a gift from the Lord; they are a reward from him" (Psalm 127:3).
- "And you yourself must be an example to them by doing good works of every kind. Let everything you do reflect the integrity and seriousness of your teaching. Teach the truth so that your teaching can't be criticized. Then those who oppose us will be ashamed and have nothing bad to say about us" (Titus 2:7-8).
- "And what do you benefit if you gain the whole world but lose your own soul? Is anything worth more than your soul" (Mark 8:36-37).

35

A Fork in the Road

HALL OF FAME BASEBALL LEGEND Yogi Berra, known for his quirky phrases, once said, "When you come to a fork in the road, take it."[5] While it was meant to be a lighthearted quip, what Berra was describing is a serious dilemma we have all faced. Have you ever been conflicted about which path was the right one to follow?

Take, for example, the career choices that plague many men throughout a wide variety of professions. Perhaps there is a new job opportunity that involves doing something you love. The position would best utilize your gifts and provide immense personal satisfaction. Sounds like an easy choice, right? Well, what if that same job opening meant a sharp reduction in salary?

Alternatively, you could stay in your current position with better financial stability, but the work is unfulfilling, even on the best of days. It seems no matter which way you go, there is a downside. Thankfully, there is a playbook to best navigate these predicaments.

Throughout the New Testament, Jesus teaches us to pray about all things both big and small. He describes Himself as the Vine and us as the branches (John 15:1-17). Only by staying connected will we enjoy the fruits. Too often, though, we as men refrain from bothering God

---

5 Garson O'Toole, "When You Come to a Fork in the Road, Take It," Quote Investigator, July 25, 2013, https://quoteinvestigator.com/2013/07/25/fork-road/#google_vignette.

with issues pertaining to our professional lives. Instead of asking for help, we dig deeper into our strengths to uncover solutions. We remain tight-lipped, holding onto our prayers as if they are in short supply. This does not yield reward but only finds us isolated in an even bigger ditch.

If praying is not something that comes easily to you, try starting each morning with the Lord's Prayer. Do this mindfully by saying it slowly and meditating on each word. As you grow more comfortable in your prayer life, you can work toward being very specific with what you are believing for. Trusting God in this way takes faith. In doing so, He will give you the direction you need today and go before you to make a way.

Key Thought: To align your heart and mind with God's purpose for you, ask for His guidance in all areas of your life. We all stray from the right path, but if we walk with faith, setbacks can become setups for a comeback.

Additional Reading:

- "'Yes, I am the vine; you are the branches. Those who remain in me, and I in them, will produce much fruit. For apart from me you can do nothing'" (John 15:5).
- "If you need wisdom, ask our generous God, and he will give it to you. He will not rebuke you for asking" (James 1:5).
- "Pray like this: Our Father in heaven, may your name be kept holy. May your Kingdom come soon. May your will

be done on earth, as it is in heaven. Give us today the food we need, and forgive us our sins, as we have forgiven those who sin against us. And don't let us yield to temptation, but rescue us from the evil one" (Matt. 6:9-13).
- "Pray in the Spirit at all times and on every occasion. Stay alert and be persistent in your prayers for all believers everywhere" (Eph. 6:18).

36

Restructuring the Org Chart

IF YOU HAVE BEEN PART of the workforce long enough, you have likely encountered a boss who was impossible to please. A few characteristics of this management style include unreasonable deadlines, poor communication, and a lack of recognition for your hard work. In more serious instances, it involves inconsiderate and even rude behavior. When this continues for months or years, it leaves us to wonder why we are bothering at all.

For some, the simple solution is to look for another job. Considering how widespread the problem is, though, you may find the same issues elsewhere. In November 2021, for example, a staggering 4.5 million people in the United States left their jobs.[6] The main cause of this turnover was not salary-related but rather the manager's poor conduct. This data provides a clear indication that it is time to shake things up at the highest level.

Think about who is currently seated at the helm of your organizational chart. If it is not God, your job satisfaction will fluctuate as wildly as the boss' mood. By changing leadership in your

---

6   Anneken Tappe, "A record 4.5 million Americans quit their jobs in November," CNN online, January 4, 2022, https://edition.cnn.com/2022/01/04/economy/us-job-openings-november/index.html.

heart, your actions fall into alignment with His purpose for you. Instead of griping, "I have to go to work today," your perspective will shift to a mentality that says, "I get to." And should your efforts go unnoticed at the office, you will be fulfilled by knowing you served God to the best of your ability.

Key Thought: When you honor God in your approach to work responsibilities, you will find meaning in even the most challenging of tasks. In living boldly without fear, you separate yourself from the pack and shine for all to see.

Additional Reading:
- "Work willingly at whatever you do, as though you were working for the Lord rather than for people. Remember that the Lord will give you an inheritance as your reward, and that the Master you are serving is Christ" (Col. 3:23-24).
- "Unless the Lord builds a house, the work of the builders is wasted. Unless the Lord protects a city, guarding it with sentries will do no good" (Psalm 127:1).
- "And may the Lord our God show us his approval and make our efforts successful. Yes, make our efforts successful" (Psalm 90:17).
- "'But don't be so concerned about perishable things like food. Spend your energy seeking the eternal life that the Son of Man can give you. For God the Father has given me the seal of his approval'" (John 6:27).

Collaborating with God

GOD IS THE ULTIMATE ARTIST, and yet His canvas has an interactive quality to it. We were made in His image, meaning we are all creators of some kind. It is our responsibility to apply these gifts to the majestic tapestry of life. Of course, we cannot all paint with the skill of Michelangelo or sing with the likes of Andrea Bocelli. Instead, there is likely another talent that is specific to you.

Maybe it is fixing cars, woodworking, building things, taking photos, playing guitar, cooking, or writing. Even though these are all quite different skill sets, they are joined by a common thread. They make the world a better place for others while also fulfilling God-given ability. That may sound like a bold proclamation for our simple hobbies, but try to look at it through a spiritual lens. You have the Divine power of creativity inside you, and it is unique from anyone else's. By sharing your gifts, God is glorified.

As men, we often put our financial obligations first, shelving any pursuits that do not generate income. While this commitment is commendable, it is important to step back and look at the bigger picture. Our goal is not to become what society expects but who God made us to be. The Creator of life as we know it has designed us to collaborate with Him. Instead of stifling our creative flair, it is time to let it shine for all to see.

Key Thought: God's Kingdom is vast with ample room for your creative contributions. Schedule time for your artistic pursuits each week. Not only will you enjoy it, but you will also be glorifying God in the process.

Additional Reading:
- "So God created human beings in his own image. In the image of God he created them; male and female he created them" (Gen. 1:27).
- "And yet, O Lord, you are our Father. We are the clay, and you are the potter. We all are formed by your hand" (Isa. 64:8).
- "The Lord has filled Bezalel with the Spirit of God, giving him great wisdom, ability, and expertise in all kinds of crafts" (Exod. 35:31).
- "Do not neglect the spiritual gift you received through the prophecy spoken over you when the elders of the church laid their hands on you" (1 Tim. 4:14).

The Recovering People-pleaser

AS CHILDREN, WE ARE NOT initially graded on math, reading, or writing. Success at this early stage of life is typically measured by how well we get along with others. Well-meaning parents reinforce this by frequently asking their kids if they made any new friends at school. All of this inadvertently puts a heavy emphasis on one's ability to fit in and be liked. From a young age, we learn ways to become an accepted part of the group.

This longing for worthiness continues into our adult years; only at this point, it is done on a bigger stage. It appears in a work setting, with in-laws, family, social circles, intimate relationships, and beyond. Yet sometimes the recognition does not come, leaving us with a feeling of inadequacy. Trying harder only exacerbates the situation. Over time, our actions become more about pleasing others than being the men God called us to be.

The fact is, you will never be enough in the eyes of everyone around you. This is not a reflection of your shortcomings, but theirs. Even Jesus, Who led a perfect, sinless life, was mocked, condemned, and ultimately put to death. He did not back down from this reality but willingly laid down His life to fulfill God's plan. This level of faithfulness is a powerful example of where we should focus our efforts.

As Christian men, we, too, will be ostracized and misunderstood. Yet if we aim to please God above all else, He promises to deliver us to eternal glory with Jesus at His mighty right hand. And while He is the only true Judge, there is nothing about your life that disqualifies you from His love. God knows the best and worst parts of your story, and He still redeems all who repent and place their faith in Him. It is in this relationship that we find where we truly belong.

Key Thought: God is on your side, and that is all you need to shine. Aim to please the Lord, and He will put everything in its right place.

Additional Reading:

- "See how very much our Father loves us, for he calls us his children, and that is what we are! But the people who belong to this world don't recognize that we are God's children because they don't know him" (1 John 3:1).
- "And may you have the power to understand, as all God's people should, how wide, how long, how high, and how deep his love is" (Eph. 3:18).
- "Even though Jesus was God's Son, he learned obedience from the things he suffered. In this way, God qualified him as a perfect High Priest, and he

became the source of eternal salvation for all those who obey him" (Heb. 5:8-9).
- "Try to please them all the time, not just when they are watching you. As slaves of Christ, do the will of God with all your heart" (Eph. 6:6).

Accepting Praise Gracefully

MANY OF US GREW UP without ever learning how to accept praise from others. Whether because we were rarely applauded or had overly critical parents, we simply did not develop this skill. Later in life, we squirm with discomfort upon receiving a well-deserved compliment. We often deflect these comments by quickly putting the focus back on the other party. Many downplay these interactions altogether and disparage their complimented efforts as "no big deal." In doing so, those who deliver the kind sentiments are not acknowledged. Worse yet, we miss a chance to glorify God for what He has done in our lives.

This process can be particularly challenging for Christian men who feel that only God is deserving of praise. While we definitely should seek to honor Him, there is an important distinction to note. Accepting a compliment is an act of humility, not pride. When someone speaks highly of your actions, it is a positive sign that you have become the person God made you to be. By simply saying, "Thanks, that means a lot to me," you are tipping your hat to the Lord.

This is not placing yourself on a pedestal but Him instead. It also offers you a unique opportunity to share what He has done in your life. If you once felt worthless, broken, and afraid, but have overcome it with God's help, that is a powerful testimony. Let others know how Jesus broke the chains, healed your wounds, and set you free. Now, the praise originally directed at you will be giving Him the glory.

Changing old habits like this takes a good deal of practice and will not happen overnight. Start by simply saying thank you the next time someone offers you positive feedback. Resist the urge to fall back into your self-deprecating ways or retort with a compliment of your own. Just accept it with humility, and remember who helped you achieve it. Over time, you will be better able to expand upon how He is using your success as part of a much greater story.

KEY THOUGHT: Accepting praise for your efforts is not putting yourself above God but showing gratitude for how He is working in your life.

ADDITIONAL READING:
- "I am so glad that you always keep me in your thoughts, and that you are following the teachings I passed on to you" (1 Cor. 11:2).
- "Whatever is good and perfect is a gift coming down to us from God our Father, who created all the lights in the heavens. He never changes or casts a shifting shadow" (James 1:17).
- "Your unfailing love is better than life itself; how I praise you" (Psalm 63:3).
- "As for human praise, we have never sought it from you or anyone else" (1 Thess. 2:6).

40
Calling Time-out

FOR A COUPLE OF FOOTBALL seasons, I spent the majority of Sundays lounging about watching the games. This all changed when I became a homeowner. Any free time was reallocated to house repairs and yard maintenance. Similarly, before I had kids, I could kick back and take in a full nine innings of baseball. These days, though, the main events on TV are usually nursery rhymes. Evenings revolve around feeding, bathtime, changing diapers, and brushing teeth. As all parents can attest, this is sometimes a real battle.

Add to this a full-time job, spouse, errands, school holidays, extended family obligations, and the frequent illnesses that kids seem to attract, and suddenly the walls of personal space close in around us. And while all of these responsibilities are indeed blessings, they can effectively eliminate our opportunity to rest. For a while, I felt guilty to admit that I even needed downtime. I mean, the house and family were something I prayed for. So, why, then, was I feeling so edgy?

Yet if you look at these first two paragraphs, you will notice something is missing. Without God, tension starts to brew. Resting in Him is the only way to stop it from boiling over.

In looking at Jesus' life, we see that even the Son of Man needed to take time for Himself. In countless stories, we read how He goes off alone to spend time with His Father. And if you look a bit closer at the timing, this usually occurs after He works tirelessly to serve others. Whether healing people, feeding the five thousand, or teaching the disciples, Jesus gave of Himself until the point of exhaustion. He needed to recharge, and this was done by leaving everyone behind and praying. Upon returning, He was filled up and ready to fulfill God's will.

Key Thought: To be solid Christian men, we need to set some boundaries and make time for rest. Even the most giving among us will start to shun others if left too depleted.

Additional Reading:
- "But Jesus often withdrew to the wilderness for prayer" (Luke 5:16).
- "After sending them home, he went up into the hills by himself to pray. Night fell while he was there alone" (Matt. 14:23).
- "Before daybreak the next morning, Jesus got up and went out to an isolated place to pray" (Mark 1:35).
- "On the seventh day God had finished his work of creation, so he rested from all his work" (Gen. 2:2).

Signs and Wonders

JESUS RARELY USED THE WORD "miracle" to explain His Divine acts. The term is scarcely mentioned in the New Testament. Instead, we find the phrase "signs and wonders." This term represents more than just word semantics; it indicates deliberate decisions. Why is this phrasing so significant?

For starters, a miracle is something that defies reason. It is a supernatural event that goes beyond natural or scientific explanation. In Jesus' short thirty-three years on earth, He proved to be far more intentional than this. Every sign He offered was designed to point us in the right direction. When we turn from sin and draw near to Him in our wonder and awe, God's will is accomplished.

If you look carefully at Scripture, it is possible to see yourself in the stories of those He healed. Have you ever lacked vision, become paralyzed with fear, been ashamed of your past, or been treated as an outcast by society? If you answered yes to any of these, Jesus left a trail of signs that leads back to Him. He let the blind see and the crippled walk. Shame was removed, and the sick were healed. These signs and wonders were performed so that we may believe. This is the loving nature of the God we serve.

Why, then, is there all this talk of miracles in Christianity? You only need to look in the mirror for the answer. You were created in

His image to live out a Divine purpose. It is in this knowledge we see God's existence in each one of us. You may be poor, weak, sick, or afflicted; but that is not where your identity lies. Through Christ alone, we discover that our destiny is to live in eternal glory with Him. It is here we come to find the most miraculous truth of all.

Key Thought: The miraculous events that have occurred throughout your life are not a mere coincidence but signs of Jesus' undying love for you. Praise God for these works, as they were intended to bring you closer to Him.

Additional Reading:
- "Jesus asked, 'Will you never believe in me unless you see miraculous signs and wonders'" (John 4:48).
- "But these are written so that you may continue to believe that Jesus is the Messiah, the Son of God, and that by believing in him you will have life by the power of his name" (John 20:31).
- "For we are God's masterpiece. He has created us anew in Christ Jesus, so we can do the good things he planned for us long ago" (Eph. 2:10).
- "Father, I want these whom you have given me to be with me where I am. Then they can see all the glory you gave me because you loved me even before the world began" (John 17:24).

42

What Has God Done for Me Lately?

THE DRIVER KILLED THE ENGINE and brought our pontoon to a halt. It was Iceland, and our tour group had front-row seats to witness large slabs of ice breaking away from a glacier. Each piece echoed as it separated from the mountain. One by one, arctic blue shards plunged into the lagoon with thunderous force. An eerie silence followed, and we watched large portions of the glacier vanish into the salty sea. "If only people who are skeptical of climate change could see this," I thought, "then they would believe." Yet today, even with rapidly increasing water temperatures, rising sea levels, and a massive increase in damaging storms, climate change remains a hotly contested topic.

It is not a big reach to apply this same concept to matters of faith. There are countless examples of God revealing Himself in the Bible, only to be later met with more pushback. Perhaps most notable is the story of Moses in the book of Exodus. Even after God saved the Israelites by parting the Red Sea, they began to question His faithfulness just forty-five days later. Despite this, more miracles followed, and they were provided with bread from the sky and good drinking water. God's glory appeared to them in the clouds above. Still, they wondered if the Lord was with them or not.

While thousands of years have passed since then, God continues to move in miraculous ways. Think back on your own life, and you will undoubtedly find notable occurrences that are hard to explain. Have there been times you were spared from injury or death, blessed with an abundance of provision at precisely the right time, or healed in a way that defied medical explanation? Perhaps you even praised Jesus in the days to follow. Like the Israelites, though, when new challenges arise, we wonder what God has done for us lately.

God knows that in the absence of constant visible reminders, we quickly fall back to our doubting ways. This is why He instructs Moses to preserve some manna in a jar for future generations to see. In this, we find a clue of how to best proceed in our modern world. Perhaps it is a glass jar you will fill with answered prayers and the supernatural ways God has acted on your behalf. Maybe it is an easily accessible list on your smartphone. Whatever method you decide to use, it should be something you can reflect on every day. When examples of God's faithfulness are on display in this tangible form, you will be hard-pressed to doubt His intentions for your current situation.

KEY THOUGHT: Trusting in God's constant presence is not always easy, especially when things are not going our way. Find a place to keep His long list of faithful measures somewhere outside of your mind. When doubt rears its head, you will have a visual reminder of His everlasting love.

ADDITIONAL READING:

- "Then Moses said, 'This is what the Lord has commanded: Fill a two-quart container with manna to preserve it for your descendants. Then later generations will be able to see the food I gave you in the wilderness when I set you free from Egypt'" (Exod. 16:32).
- "Never let loyalty and kindness leave you! Tie them around your neck as a reminder. Write them deep within your heart" (Prov. 3:3).
- "Jesus also did many other things. If they were all written down, I suppose the whole world could not contain the books that would be written" (John 21:25).
- "Yes, and the Lord will deliver me from every evil attack and will bring me safely into his heavenly Kingdom. All glory to God forever and ever! Amen" (2 Tim. 4:18).

43

Being Chosen

IF YOUR CHILDHOOD INVOLVED ANY schoolyard sports, you likely experienced the time-honored tradition of being picked for a team. One by one, each captain chose whom they wanted to play on their squad. Of course, it was always the most accomplished athletes who were called upon first. By the last round, the only remaining kids were those lacking in physical gifts. And while they made the team by default, they were left feeling rather inadequate.

In God's Kingdom, it is those who have always been last who are put first. This does not mean Heaven is filled with unathletic believers. More accurately, God uses our limitations to bring Him the ultimate glory. If you were voted "least likely to succeed" in your school's yearbook, God can turn that on its head.

Maybe you do not feel worthy, or perhaps you have never felt good enough; but to Jesus, it is those who are marginalized who are the most important. He has prepared a place for you to thrive in His love, grace, and mercy. It is in our weakness that we are made strong. From suffering, there is peace. Out of pain, comes healing. And from brokenness, redemption.

Recognize the value of your perceived shortcomings, as it helps to frame them with a heavenly perspective. What are some of the challenges and failures you have experienced? List them, and consider how they can be used to help uplift others who may be struggling with something similar. You may think of your shortcomings as a flaw, but God views them as an opportunity. Through this process, you will discover how those days of finishing last were preparing you for something far greater.

> Key Thought: As the Author of our faith, God uses the unfinished ends to write a new beginning. The traits we once considered undesirable will prove victorious in revealing His glory.

Additional Reading:
- "'So those who are last now will be first then, and those who are first will be last'" (Matt. 20:16).
- "But the Lord said to Samuel, 'Don't judge by his appearance or height, for I have rejected him. The Lord doesn't see things the way you see them. People judge by outward appearance, but the Lord looks at the heart'" (1 Sam. 16:7).
- "In his kindness God called you to share in his eternal glory by means of Christ Jesus. So after you have suffered a little while, he will restore, support, and strengthen you, and he will place you on a firm foundation" (1 Peter 5:10).
- "We do this by keeping our eyes on Jesus, the champion who initiates and perfects our faith. Because of the joy awaiting him, he endured the cross, disregarding its shame. Now he is seated in the place of honor beside God's throne" (Heb. 12:2).

44
It Is Not the Size That Matters

DESPITE WHAT SOCIAL MEDIA NETWORKS may claim, their services are no longer just a fun place to scroll through photos, videos, and memes. Over the last several years, these apps have seemingly become an integral part of people's identity and worth. Providing links to your profiles is now required on certain job applications and even paperwork for travel visas. To secure a professional contract, artists, authors, and public speakers (myself included) are often asked about the size of their platform. It seems that the number of accrued followers is used to measure how qualified someone is. This mistakenly omits one very important distinction: God gives each one of us the appropriately sized launching pad to accomplish the work He has called us to.

Rather than falling victim to the current obsession with gaining followers, we need to focus on being devoted followers to just one, Christ Jesus. The alternative is a prideful pursuit of inflated stats that offer no real benefit. It is now even possible to pay for followers, but at what cost to your soul? This only feeds into the rat race in which no one ever wins. A more fruitful approach is to focus our efforts solely on pleasing God. Only with this heart of surrender can we become the person He has destined us to be.

Take a look at the stories and posts you have published previously. Do they glorify what God is doing in your life, or are they merely a highlight reel boasting about your achievements? If it is the latter, you have a real opportunity to grow in ways that transcend social media.

The algorithms of these platforms do not typically reward those who are humble. Instead, it is the updates that cause controversy or divisiveness that receive the most notoriety. These methods may even bring momentary fame; but if the success is not founded in God's will, it will be short-lived. The news is filled with tales of public figures who unceremoniously tumbled from their pedestal in ruin. As men of faith, we must look beyond the trending hashtags and align ourselves with the eternal.

For some, this may involve taking a thirty-day hiatus from social media. Others may find a better balance by setting daily screen time limits. Perhaps the most God-centered approach is to use these sites as a tool to share your walk of faith to encourage others. You may lose a few followers along the way, but what God's Kingdom gains is far greater than these numbers can quantify.

KEY THOUGHT: As a society, we spend an inordinate amount of time, money, and effort on gaining followers. Meanwhile, the platform we seek has already been promised by God. We only need to follow Him to find true success.

ADDITIONAL READING:
- "Seek the Kingdom of God above all else, and he will give you everything you need" (Luke 12:31).
- "'You must not have any other god but me'" (Deut. 5:7)
- "Fools have no interest in understanding; they only want to air their own opinions" (Prov. 18:2).
- "He must become greater and greater, and I must become less and less" (John 3:30).

45
WRESTLING WITH GOD

IN PROFESSIONAL WRESTLING, ONE OF the more popular characters wields a devastating move called "the AA." This powerful maneuver drives the opponent's back into the mat with brutal force. In the opponent's defeat, their once prideful persona is humbled. And with this, they experience the aptly named "attitude adjustment."

While the stunts mentioned above are meant for entertainment, there is a metaphor for spiritual truth here. We are called to walk with a submissive frame of mind. This is not to suggest that God should hoist us over His massive shoulders and slam us down. More accurately, He wants to mend our souls through His love.

In the inspiring movie *Facing the Giants*, the coach tells his players, "Your attitude is like the aroma of your heart; if your attitude stinks, it means your heart is not right."[7] If we are being honest, all of us have experienced this at one time or another. We complain when things do not go our way and grumble at tasks we would rather not take on. Rather than surrendering to God's will, we wrestle with Him.

To develop a strong reliance on God, we need to tackle the challenges set before us with a joyful heart. Sure, some of it will be difficult, even painful. Yet God puts seemingly impossible obstacles in front of us so we can learn to lean on Him. This builds character,

---

7   Alex Kendrick, *Facing the Giants* (2006, Culver City: Destination Films), DVD.

perseverance, and hope. As your trust grows, the grumbles will soon be replaced by praise.

KEY THOUGHT: An optimistic attitude is all too often the overlooked seed needed to grow abundant joy. Instead of wrestling with God, join forces to become the best version of yourself.

ADDITIONAL READING:

- "I know how to live on almost nothing or with everything. I have learned the secret of living in every situation, whether it is with a full stomach or empty, with plenty or little. For I can do everything through Christ, who gives me strength" (Phil. 4:12-13).
- "Yes, this anguish was good for me, for you have rescued me from death and forgiven all my sins" (Isa. 38:17).
- "My God! Now I am deeply discouraged, but I will remember you—even from distant Mount Hermon, the source of the Jordan, from the land of Mount Mizar" (Psalm 42:6).
- "This is the day the Lord has made. We will rejoice and be glad in it" (Psalm 118:24).

46

GAINING CONTROL BY LETTING GO

IN THE HISTORY OF MAJOR League Baseball, only thirty-four pitchers are recorded as being "knuckleballers."[8] This extremely small number is due to how difficult the mysterious pitch—the knuckleball—is to master. The art of throwing it successfully requires the pitcher to use a light grip on the ball. Arm strength and velocity are not paramount to doing it well. The main goal is to limit the amount of spin and rotation on the ball once it leaves your hand. It is essentially the complete opposite of the traditional mechanics being taught around the world.

If that all sounds a bit too complicated, there is one major benefit of a knuckleball. When it is thrown properly, it is virtually impossible to hit. Even professional catchers wear a special oversized glove to improve their likelihood of catching it. This makes it great fun for spectators to watch, but it also highlights an important biblical principle.

Only by relinquishing control and trusting God's will can we enjoy the peace of mind we so desperately seek. Trying to sway

---

8   "List of knuckleball pitchers," Wikimedia Foundation, last modified June 29, 2023, https://en.wikipedia.org/wiki/List_of_knuckleball_pitchers.

situations with a vicelike grip is doing us a disservice. The tighter we hold on, the more things spin out of orbit.

God works in ways that surpass all earthly understanding. Our limited human capacity cannot possibly compare to the elaborate plans He has for our lives. Throughout the Bible, God promises to never leave us and to provide what we need most. Just as you would do anything possible to help your children, so, too, would He with you. Just remember, God can only lead us if we are willing to follow.

Trusting God in this way takes practice. To do so, it can be helpful to start with smaller prayers. Maybe you are not ready to say, "Use me however You see fit." Instead, try something like, "Please, Lord, remind me of all the ways You have helped me in the past so that I can stop holding on so tight and grow my trust in You."

Key Thought: The tangles of life that once made little sense will one day form a clearer picture. By letting go, you stop looking inward for the answers and seek His will instead.

Additional Reading:
- "Trust in the Lord with all your heart; do not depend on your own understanding. Seek his will in all you do, and he will show you which path to take" (Prov. 3:5-6).
- "For the Lord your God is a merciful God; he will not abandon you or destroy you or forget the solemn covenant he made with your ancestors" (Deut. 4:31).

- "So if you sinful people know how to give good gifts to your children, how much more will your heavenly Father give good gifts to those who ask him" (Matt. 7:11).
- "The faithful love of the Lord never ends! His mercies never cease. Great is his faithfulness; his mercies begin afresh each morning" (Lam. 3:22-23).

47

Fueled by God

IMAGINE NOT BEING ABLE TO see your knees beneath an increasingly bulging belly. I can tell you from experience that it is anything but flattering. I have wanted to hide in a closet from embarrassment. It was not just the visible aspects that bothered me but also the blood work revealing prediabetes. Instead of honoring God with my body, I had chosen to eat ice cream sundaes, pizza, and fast food. I was destroying the temple walls and everything inside it. Without drastic measures, the whole thing would soon come tumbling down.

Like most people dealing with a health scare, I started working out diligently and changing what I ate. This helped quite a bit but not nearly as fast as one would hope. It was not until I prayed for wisdom that things started to turn around. God revealed to me that my body was a direct reflection of a deep internal struggle. I was ashamed of my life and the poor choices I had made and was harming myself with food. I essentially went to church for the bagels and cream cheese rather than the actual message. God was part of my days but was certainly not the Lord of my life.

I made a vow to do my best and let God do the rest. It was while sweating on the treadmill that God started to move. The extra pounds were falling away, but that was not the only transformation. What once was shame turned into redemption. My weakness had become a strength, and fear was replaced by courage. I was no longer a victim but an overcomer. What initially appeared as a fast track to an early grave became a launching pad for a future fueled by God.

Key Thought: Our bodies are a reflection of how we view ourselves deep within. If you are struggling with your image, look to God for clarity on just how loved you are.

Additional Reading:
- "For God bought you with a high price. So you must honor God with your body" (1 Cor. 6:20).
- "'Physical training is good, but training for godliness is much better, promising benefits in this life and in the life to come'" (1 Tim. 4:8).
- "Don't copy the behavior and customs of this world, but let God transform you into a new person by changing the way you think. Then you will learn to know God's will for you, which is good and pleasing and perfect" (Rom. 12:2).
- "'Your eye is like a lamp that provides light for your body. When your eye is healthy, your whole body is filled with light'" (Matt. 6:22).

48

GETTING STARTED

AFTER MONTHS OF HARD TRAINING, the big race was just days away. It was to be my first marathon, yet I was anything but excited. This was not just ordinary cold feet but crippling self-doubt.

On my last few training runs, the thought of quitting was all-consuming. I told myself that I simply did not have what it takes. In my mind echoed phrases like, "I have failed so many times before in my life—what makes this any different?" The thought of crossing the finish line seemed impossible. I was on the verge of skipping the required athlete check-in process altogether. Doing so would essentially disqualify me from even starting the race.

That same morning, a family friend biked down our street. When she reached the corner, a voice inside told her to turn around and come back. Not knowing where we lived, she happened to pedal past our driveway. There she saw our child playing in the yard. She came inside to find me overwhelmed and mentally defeated. "I got a message that I am supposed to be here," she said.

Just a week earlier, I had seen this same friend walking with arm braces. The pain from an old spinal injury had been excruciating. Yet here she was with a smile on her face and a word of encouragement. Despite her very real struggles, she had recently placed her trust in Jesus. I knew what I had to do and vowed to check myself in for the event.

The actual race was admittedly challenging. I accidentally kicked a curb and broke my big toe halfway through the distance. Pain permeated through my entire foot. Yet as the kilometers ticked by, I thought about the story of Peter in Matthew 14:28-31. He walked on water in a storm to reach Jesus. He was doing the impossible! It was only when he took his eyes off Jesus to look at the surrounding danger that he started to sink. "Jesus immediately reached out and grabbed him. 'You have so little faith,' Jesus said. 'Why did you doubt me?'" (Matt. 14:31).

I began to pray out loud. "Lord, I need Your help now to finish this race, just as I need You in everyday life." When I crossed the finish line and pointed toward the heavens, it was an acknowledgment that the victory was not mine. All the glory was God's. He put the right people in my life at the most opportune time to complete His work in me. When my limited earthly power came to an end, His was just getting started.

Key Thought: Rather than looking at how far you have come or how much further there is to go, keep your sights set on Him. Trust God to help you finish the race, even in your weakest moments.

Additional Reading:
- "My health may fail, and my spirit may grow weak, but God remains the strength of my heart; he is mine forever" (Psalm 73:26).
- "Therefore, since we are surrounded by such a huge crowd of witnesses to the life of faith, let us strip off

every weight that slows us down, especially the sin that so easily trips us up. And let us run with endurance the race God has set before us" (Heb. 12:1).

- "Each time he said, 'My grace is all you need. My power works best in weakness.' So now I am glad to boast about my weaknesses, so that the power of Christ can work through me" (2 Cor. 12:9).
- "So let's not get tired of doing what is good. At just the right time we will reap a harvest of blessing if we don't give up" (Gal. 6:9).

49
SHIELDED BY SCRIPTURE

AFTER FORTY DAYS OF FASTING in the desert, Jesus was tested by the devil. The timing here is noteworthy as Jesus was physically hungry and therefore more vulnerable to attack. Despite this, Jesus successfully wards off each manipulative attempt. He accomplished this not through brute force but with Scripture. In each of His three rebuttals, Jesus says, "The Scriptures say" and proceeds to quote a verse from the book of Deuteronomy (Matt. 4:1-11).

For many Christians, the Old Testament is a challenging read. Some shy away from it altogether, choosing to focus only on Jesus and the New Testament. In fairness, there are portions of the Old Testament that are hard to follow. Yet the Son of God shows us just how powerful this part of Scripture is. In fact, it was so effective that the devil had no choice but to give up and flee.

A great deal of insight can be gained from this confrontation between Jesus and the devil. Satan first attacks Jesus by attempting to paint Him as prideful. He goes on to remind Jesus of the uncomfortable feeling of being hungry. Next, he questions Jesus' holiness and tries to have Him test God's faithfulness. Finally, he tempts Jesus with promises of riches and power. Do any of these tactics sound familiar from your own life? Jesus teaches us how to fend off these strikes and walk away unscathed.

Before you get started, while reading the Bible from cover to cover has its advantages, there are other more accessible approaches. One alternative is to try a web search with a topic you are currently struggling with and the word "Bible" at the end. For example, browse for "struggles with temptation Bible." You will notice over 15,200,000 results. The first page will be filled with applicable verses to write on the tablet of your heart. Of course, there are also daily devotionals and other bite-sized applications to absorb the Word. Whatever way fits you best, He will be right there in the midst of it.

KEY THOUGHT: By looking carefully at how the devil tries to tempt Jesus, we can find many parallels to our own lives. Take time to highlight some verses that can be called on when you need them most.

ADDITIONAL READING:
- "Such things were written in the Scriptures long ago to teach us. And the Scriptures give us hope and encouragement as we wait patiently for God's promises to be fulfilled" (Rom. 15:4).
- "Obey my commands and live! Guard my instructions as you guard your own eyes. Tie them on your fingers as a reminder. Write them deep within your heart" (Prov. 7:2-3).
- "But Jesus told him, 'No! The Scriptures say, *People do not live by bread alone, but by every word that comes from the mouth of God*'" (Matt. 4:4).
- "So humble yourselves before God. Resist the devil, and he will flee from you" (James 4:7).

Positioned for Success

SHORTLY AFTER MOVING FROM NEW York to New Zealand, I had an opportunity to watch a cricket match. Kiwis are passionate about their sporting events, and I tried to figure out what all the fuss was about. To say I was highly confused would be an understatement. There were a few similarities to baseball, but the positioning of the players was quite different from anything I had seen before.

With time and some patient explanations from friends, the strategic aspects of the game started to make sense. The active playing field is 360 degrees. Whether you are batting or fielding, success is largely determined by how you analyze and use field placement. All it takes is a single error in judgment for one team to take advantage and run up the score.

In our own lives, we sometimes feel grossly out of place. Maybe you have moved to a new city, state, or country. Perhaps you are struggling to find peace within yourself or are facing a challenging relationship, a different job, church, or community. During these seasons, we wonder if God somehow missed the mark and left us where we do not belong.

Jesus knew we would ponder these questions and promises that through faith in Him, we will see victory. He invites us to rest easy and remain confident that we have been positioned in exactly the right place. Of course, during our most profound struggles, this can be rather difficult to do. Yet God is the ultimate Strategist, guiding our movements to fulfill His purpose in our life. What initially seems like failure is setting you up for the next success.

Key Thought: God's vast story is one of redemption. We may lose a few matches along the way' but in doing so, we are better positioned for the next win. The obstacles that once appeared as roadblocks will soon be revealed as guardrails that helped guide you to a better place.

Additional Reading:
- "For every child of God defeats this evil world, and we achieve this victory through our faith" (1 John 5:4).
- "Then Jesus said, 'Come to me, all of you who are weary and carry heavy burdens, and I will give you rest. Take my yoke upon you. Let me teach you, because I am humble and gentle at heart, and you will find rest for your souls. For my yoke is easy to bear, and the burden I give you is light'" (Matt. 11:28-30).
- "'For I know the plans I have for you,' says the Lord. 'They are plans for good and not for disaster, to give you a future and a hope'" (Jer. 29:11).
- "But thank God! He gives us victory over sin and death through our Lord Jesus Christ" (1 Cor. 15:57).

51

Shame Unmasked

THE FIRST DAY TERRENCE WALKED into the church, he was a man shrouded in mystery. His face lay hidden behind a COVID mask and hooded sweatshirt. Sitting in the back pew, he listened quietly and kept to himself. After the last song finished and the service ended, he made a quick exit. Yet right before leaving, he stopped to thank the youth group leader.

He explained how his fourteen-year-old son had been attending the youth group and how he had changed for the better as a result. Like many teens, the boy had been struggling to find direction and meaning in his life. Now, he seemed more outgoing, happier, and at peace.

The very next week, Terrence was back but did not quite look the same. The mask-wearing protocol had since changed. Now, without anything to obscure his face, a series of gang tattoos were clearly visible. Yet there was something else that was different. It was only after we talked that the difference became apparent: "Last week I came for my son; today I came for me." That same evening, Terrence gave his heart to the Lord. His story would later bring me to weep.

God longs for a relationship with all of His children regardless of our past. When we run from Him, He searches for ways to reach us. This is sometimes done through the people placed in our lives or the situations He presents to us. In Terrence's case, it was his son's faith that opened the door for Jesus to work in both of their lives. We can hide our faces in shame, but He sees us for who we truly are and stops at nothing to bring us back home.

KEY THOUGHT: When we place our faith in Jesus and ask for forgiveness, He casts light upon the darkest areas of our lives and uses it for good.

ADDITIONAL READING:
- "I can never escape from your Spirit! I can never get away from your presence! If I go up to heaven, you are there; if I go down to the grave, you are there" (Psalm 139:7-8).
- "Those who look to him for help will be radiant with joy; no shadow of shame will darken their faces" (Psalm 34:5).
- "But when the teachers of religious law who were Pharisees saw him eating with tax collectors and other sinners, they asked his disciples, 'Why does he eat with such scum?' When Jesus heard this, he told them, 'Healthy people don't need a doctor—sick people do. I have come to call not those who think they are righteous, but those who know they are sinners'" (Mark 2:16-17).
- "But if we confess our sins to him, he is faithful and just to forgive us our sins and to cleanse us from all wickedness" (1 John 1:9).

WHEN QUITTING IS ESSENTIAL

SOME BELIEVE THAT SIN IS a positive thing if it eventually leads us closer to God. While it is a deep and interesting thought, it sidesteps an important fact from the Bible. God desperately wants us to quit our sinning ways right now. And while He does forgive our wrongdoing, the cost was Jesus' life. When you look at it this way, it becomes clear that God's grace is the transformative element, not sin.

Despite the unimaginable suffering Jesus was about to endure on the cross, He prayed for us as believers. He desired that we live in unity with Him and those around us. Yet in society, we hear phrases like, "It is better to ask for forgiveness than to seek permission." While this may work in a corporate setting, it does not translate into the spiritual realm. How can we claim to love Jesus if we do not follow His Word? "Keep my commands," He says, and you will be given the power of the Holy Spirit.

This does not mean that God expects His children to be perfect. Yet as we grow closer to Him, our iniquities become more evident. Forgiveness has been promised, but only when we truly repent. In turning from sin, we put Him over the cravings of our flesh. The reward has far greater reach than anything else we can pursue.

Key Thought: In sinning, we may satisfy our earthly impulses, but doing so distances us from God. Breaking habits and patterns from the past takes intentional effort but will yield real and lasting transformation.

Additional Reading:
- "'If you love me, obey my commandments'" (John 14:15).
- "It's your sins that have cut you off from God. Because of your sins, he has turned away and will not listen anymore" (Isa. 59:2).
- "If we claim we have no sin, we are only fooling ourselves and not living in the truth" (1 John 1:8).
- "The Lord isn't really being slow about his promise, as some people think. No, he is being patient for your sake. He does not want anyone to be destroyed, but wants everyone to repent" (2 Peter 3:9).

53
Controlled Burns

YOSEMITE NATIONAL PARK IS A true gem in America's vast network of protected lands. With iconic natural features such as Half Dome and El Capitan, it receives an average of five million awestruck visitors each year.[9] And while the thundering waterfalls and abundant wildlife have inspired generations of artists and nature enthusiasts, the park is also rife with devastating wildfires. Every summer, countless acres of pristine forests are consumed, leaving behind a barren wasteland of scorched trees.

To counter these infernos, the parks department carries out a series of controlled burns. By purposely setting fire to the old brush and downed trees, the potential burn areas are significantly reduced. The method has proven so effective that it reduces the intensity of wildfires by 76 percent.[10] In many cases, this has spared the homes and lives of nearby residents.

Over the trajectory of our complicated life journeys, we, too, can fall victim to the scattered debris of the past. If left unaddressed,

---

[9] "New Visitation Record In 2016 As Over 5 Million People Visited Yosemite National Park," Sierra Sun Times online, January 13, 2017, https://goldrush-cam.com/sierrasuntimes/index.php/news/local-news/8685-new-visitation-record-in-2016-as-over-5-million-people-visited-yosemite-national-park.

[10] "Fire operations-prescribed burning combo reduces wildfire severity up to 72%," ScienceDaily.com, July 14, 2021, www.sciencedaily.com/releases/2021/07/210714151142.htm.

old grudges, haunting regret, and earlier failures can flare up with a simple spark. We become vulnerable to people and situations capable of fanning these flames. Before long, we are engulfed in turmoil with no clear way forward.

As followers of Jesus, our story does not have to end this way. God can take the ashes of our past and turn them into something beautiful. In walking with Him, we find ourselves on fertile ground. With the old now forgiven, new life can truly take root and flourish. Consider this to be your promised land. To experience it, we must be intentional and choose to let Jesus transform the landscape of our lives.

> Key Thought: If you have been burned in the past, Jesus can use the charred remains to forge a new, more fruitful future. The next great opportunity lies just ahead of you.

Additional Reading:

- "To all who mourn in Israel, he will give a crown of beauty for ashes, a joyous blessing instead of mourning, festive praise instead of despair. In their righteousness, they will be like great oaks that the Lord has planted for his own glory" (Isa. 61:3).
- "No, dear brothers and sisters, I have not achieved it, but I focus on this one thing: Forgetting the past and looking forward to what lies ahead, I press on to reach the end of the race and receive the heavenly prize for which God, through Christ Jesus, is calling us" (Phil. 3:13-14).

- "So now there is no condemnation for those who belong to Christ Jesus. And because you belong to him, the power of the life-giving Spirit has freed you from the power of sin that leads to death" (Rom. 8:1-2).
- "So let us come boldly to the throne of our gracious God. There we will receive his mercy, and we will find grace to help us when we need it most" (Heb. 4:16).

54
From Handcuffs to Praise

HAVE YOU EVER BEEN HANDCUFFED? I have, but it was not due to a crime I committed. Ironically, it was the result of my immense dissatisfaction with life. My marriage of seven years had dissolved, and the impending divorce led to sleepless nights and panic attacks. Even with a steady diet of antidepressants, my world felt as if it was being torn apart.

Up until this point, I was driven by creating an image of perceived success and living up to someone else's standards. I worked over sixty hours a week; but my sights were always set on the next big sale, promotional opportunity, pay raise, or material acquisition. There were many problems with this, of course, including drinking too much and feeling trapped in a loveless marriage. The biggest issue, however, was that I pushed God out of the picture.

It all came to a screeching halt after an argument with my spouse. I retreated to my safe space and locked myself inside the garage. Moments later, alternating flashes of red and blue police lights illuminated the otherwise dark street. They were taking me to an inpatient mental health facility. The one catch, though, was that they needed to handcuff me first. This safety measure, as they called it, was standard protocol in such situations. With hands shackled behind my back, they ushered me into the patrol car.

After a few days in the hospital, I found myself in conversation with another patient. I asked what she was reading.

"*Jesus Calling*," she said. "Would you like to read today's passage with me?"

I paused for a few seconds, but in that instant, I could feel the tide of my life about to surge forward.

"Sure, why not?" I replied casually. With that, there was an undeniable sense of Jesus kicking down a door and pouring into my soul. It only took one small opening for Him to fill my heart with the hope of a better future.

I was baptized shortly after my discharge and have continued to grow my relationship with Jesus. Life was not perfect, but I no longer walked alone. And while my marriage was not saved, I most certainly was.

KEY THOUGHT: Surrendering your life to Jesus does not impinge on your liberty but rather sets you free.

ADDITIONAL READING:
- "There is a path before each person that seems right, but it ends in death" (Prov. 14:12).
- "For God is working in you, giving you the desire and the power to do what pleases him" (Phil. 2:13).
- "'Look! I stand at the door and knock. If you hear my voice and open the door, I will come in, and we will share a meal together as friends'" (Rev. 3:20).
- "For the Lord is the Spirit, and wherever the Spirit of the Lord is, there is freedom" (2 Cor. 3:17).

55
Spiritual Boot Camp

IF YOU HAVE WATCHED ANY movies based on the military, you are likely familiar with the drill sergeant's role. This is the person charged with shaping civilians into hardened soldiers. Standing face to face with barely an inch of separation from the recruit, the officer barks angrily to try and break their spirit. I can tell you from personal experience that this is not an exaggerated Hollywood depiction but an accurate representation of life in boot camp. What is not captured on film, though, is how God can provide joy for His children in the most unlikely situations. When we place our trust in Him, it is possible to experience deep inner peace even while under heavy attack.

Take the story of Paul and Silas, for example, in Acts 16. Before being thrown into jail, they were violently beaten with rods as the public looked on. Despite this heinous act, they sang hymns of worship from their cell while praying for all to hear. Can you imagine doing this with the very real possibility of receiving additional punishment? Yet soon after, their courageous faith was rewarded in a mighty way. An earthquake rattled the prison and broke the shackles from their arms.

In our day-to-day life, we all come up against trials that can feel just as difficult. It may not be boot camp or prison but a relationship conflict or work challenge that is weighing on your soul. Perhaps it is a financial burden or a health-related crisis. Whatever the challenge may be, Paul tells us that through faith in Jesus, we can live with a peace that surpasses all understanding (Phil. 4:7). The question is, will you choose to trust God amid these struggles or remain bound by fear?

Key Thought: Jesus set us free from the shackles that once imprisoned our souls. How will you choose to honor His sacrifice and make the most of your second chance at life?

Additional Reading:
- "Dear brothers and sisters, when troubles of any kind come your way, consider it an opportunity for great joy. For you know that when your faith is tested, your endurance has a chance to grow" (James 1:2-3).
- "Then I will hold my head high above my enemies who surround me. At his sanctuary I will offer sacrifices with shouts of joy, singing and praising the Lord with music" (Psalm 27:6).
- "Then you will experience God's peace, which exceeds anything we can understand. His peace will guard your hearts and minds as you live in Christ Jesus" (Phil. 4:7).
- "Around midnight Paul and Silas were praying and singing hymns to God, and the other prisoners were listening. Suddenly, there was a massive earthquake, and the prison was shaken to its foundations. All the doors immediately flew open, and the chains of every prisoner fell off" (Acts 16:25-26).

Relationship Over Religion

FRIENDS WHO KNOW ME WELL are often surprised when I describe my faith as more of a relationship with Jesus than religion. Do not get me wrong—following the Ten Commandments and laws outlined in the Bible can put you on a good path, but it is only part of being a Christian. And while I attend church quite regularly, that involves two hours per week at most. Statistically speaking, we spend more time than that on social media. Yet Jesus calls us to be in continuous communication with Him. Only when we stay connected in prayer throughout the week will we feel noticeably closer to God.

I was once part of a large church that operated like a well-choreographed dance company. When one service ended, the next congregation would be welcomed in the front door as the others were ushered out the back. There was little opportunity to talk with anyone in a meaningful way.

The pastor was a talented speaker who used relevant cultural events to call attention to scriptural principles. This made him quite popular; but ultimately, this turned out to be somewhat problematic. He was so well-liked that attendance dropped dramatically when he took a scheduled vacation.

The strength of your relationship with God should not depend on who is speaking on Sunday. Church services are meant to spark your curiosity and encourage you to dig deeper in your own time.

It is the conversations you have with God in between sermons that ultimately sets your heart ablaze for Him. There are scores of passages that describe how valuable we are to God. As the Shepherd of our hearts, Jesus values the transformation of one man's soul over a big church turnout of those proclaiming to be righteous. This can be put into practice in a variety of ways. A few approaches are listening to worship music, praying, appreciating God's creations in nature, studying the Word, and simply pausing to praise and give thanks for His faithfulness.

Key Thought: To make Jesus the Lord of your heart, draw close to Him each day, not just on Sundays. It is in these quiet moments with God that you gather strength and prepare to move forward positively.

Additional Reading:
- "Always be joyful. Never stop praying. Be thankful in all circumstances, for this is God's will for you who belong to Christ Jesus" (1 Thess. 5:16-18).
- "'You must not make for yourself an idol of any kind or an image of anything in the heavens or on the earth or in the sea'" (Exod. 20:4).
- "One of the teachers of religious law was standing there listening to the debate. He realized that Jesus had answered well, so he asked, 'Of all the commandments,

which is the most important?' Jesus replied, 'The most important commandment is this: *Listen, O Israel! The Lord our God is the one and only Lord'"* (Mark 12:28-29).

- "In the same way, there is more joy in heaven over one lost sinner who repents and returns to God than over ninety-nine others who are righteous and haven't strayed away" (Luke 15:7).

Exercising Faith in the Face of Doubt

LOOK AROUND THE CHURCH ON any given Sunday, and you will notice a large number of smiling faces chatting about how good God is. What is rarely mentioned, though, are the nagging doubts with which we sometimes struggle. This is particularly true for those who are processing grief, illness, and financial instability. Let us be honest, singing about God's love during these times is challenging. Even the most certain among us can wonder, "What if God does not come through for me this time?" Yet we stifle our uncertainty for fear of being dubbed a weak Christian or displeasing God.

Unfortunately, this shame causes us to miss an important truth. Doubt is only possible where some level of belief already exists. And while throughout the Bible, Jesus encourages us to grow our beliefs, He makes a powerful promise to those who are struggling. With faith the size of a tiny seed, He can move mountains in your life (Matt. 17:20). If you are currently in that place of apprehension, you are perfectly positioned for God to do something big.

As a form of spiritual exercise, start by trusting God with small things and building from there. No matter how well-written this devotional is, it cannot possibly satisfy every hesitation you may have. That peace of mind can only come from our Creator. Ask yourself, "Has God always had my back in the past?" Next, pray about your current situation and for Him to develop conviction in any areas of unbelief. Finally, look to His Word for the promises made about your future.

Key Thought: Questioning aspects of our faith is essential, but the answers we seek can only be found in God, the Source. Do not be afraid to stand tall and express your faith even when it differs from the status quo.

Additional Reading:
- "So faith comes from hearing, that is, hearing the Good News about Christ" (Rom. 10:17).
- "'Are you the Messiah we've been expecting, or should we keep looking for someone else'" (Matt. 11:3).
- "'You don't have enough faith,' Jesus told them. 'I tell you the truth, if you had faith even as small as a mustard seed, you could say to this mountain, *Move from here to there*, and it would move. Nothing would be impossible'" (Matt. 17:20).
- "And we know that God causes everything to work together for the good of those who love God and are called according to his purpose for them" (Rom. 8:28).

Dropping Cruise Control

WE ALL HAVE ASPECTS OF our lives that can be improved upon. This can be healthy to acknowledge as it propels us to growth on several fronts. The challenge is that change can be uncomfortable. It forces us into unfamiliar areas of vulnerability. As adults, we quickly discover that growing pains are not isolated to our childhood.

Eventually, we tire of the struggle and seek comfort instead. For many men, the solution is to settle into a routine, accept the situation as it is, and plow forward on cruise control. While this approach can be convenient, it limits our engagement throughout the journey. Simply going with the flow prevents us from getting on and off the highway and discovering what God has in store for us.

As most seasoned travelers will attest, it is the back roads that often lead to the most rewarding treasures. And while getting lost is sometimes frightening, it is an essential part of finding ourselves in God.

Maybe you have been cruising along for some time now and feel it is too late to leave the fast lane. Yet if not now, then when? Our time here on earth is a gift, and there is no time like the present to unwrap all God has to offer. It may be messy, but what you will find is far greater than any comfort station can provide.

KEY THOUGHT: To follow God's direction in your life requires constant adjustment, but the journey will prepare you for the final destination.

ADDITIONAL READING:
- "'His purpose was for the nations to seek after God and perhaps feel their way toward him and find him—though he is not far from any one of us'" (Acts 17:27).
- "If you look for me wholeheartedly, you will find me" (Jer. 29:13).
- "'The Kingdom of Heaven is like a treasure that a man discovered hidden in a field. In his excitement, he hid it again and sold everything he owned to get enough money to buy the field'" (Matt. 13:44).
- "He existed before anything else, and he holds all creation together" (Col. 1:17).

When Bad News Comes

HOW DO YOU RESPOND WHEN life is abruptly interrupted by tragedy? We have all received a phone call, a text, or an email that sends us reeling as if from a blow. If you have not experienced this yet, it is an inevitable part of our time on earth. I say this not to spread doom and fear but to offer space for pre-deciding your course of action. The Bible tells us that storms are not a matter of if but when.

This presents us with two choices. We can proceed with anxiety, always on edge and stressed about what is to come. Or we can recognize these tests as a unique opportunity. Just as the muscles in your body gain strength from resistance, our faith is built by the strain of life's trials. The old saying "use it or lose it" may have been intended for athletes, but it applies to our spiritual endurance as well. This is not to say that bad news will not bring you to your knees. It is in this despair that we are positioned to draw closer to God in prayer.

In sports, athletes are always working to find small adjustments that will set them apart. We, too, have an advantage to help us succeed in our race. There is nothing this world can throw at you that cannot be overcome with God by your side. Even when the odds are stacked against you, He is the Ace up your sleeve. When it feels you cannot possibly stand up to the challenge, Jesus is the Way-maker.

The Holy Spirit will deliver strength when it is required, and God will carry you if need be. Victory then is not about reaching the finish line but rather crossing it with Jesus. This is our Holy Trinity, an ever-present Force to deliver us from the devastation of a fallen world. People may tell you there is a light at the end of the tunnel. Jesus teaches that He is right there with us in the midst of the darkness. Choose to trust Him when storms gather, and you will rise to the occasion.

KEY THOUGHT: Our journey through life is riddled with devastating pits of despair. Resolve now to call upon Jesus at your lowest points, and He will see you through when you need it most.

ADDITIONAL READING:
- "They do not fear bad news; they confidently trust the Lord to care for them" (Psalm 112:7).
- "Even when I walk through the darkest valley, I will not be afraid, for you are close beside me. Your rod and your staff protect and comfort me" (Psalm 23:4).
- "Enjoy prosperity while you can, but when hard times strike, realize that both come from God. Remember that nothing is certain in this life" (Eccl. 7:14).
- "And this same God who takes care of me will supply all your needs from his glorious riches, which have been given to us in Christ Jesus" (Phil. 4:19).

60
Jesus Never Fails

I HAVE USED THE PHRASE, "It was unbelievable!" to describe many of the miraculous events I have witnessed. While proclaimed with genuine excitement, the words no longer seem to fit now that I follow Jesus. Through Him, I have learned there is nothing He cannot do for those who believe. This has come to fruition so often, I decided to remove the expression from my vocabulary altogether. One question remained: what should I replace it with?

The answer came from a wooden sign that sat atop the breakfast nook in my childhood home. Although it was small, it seemed to hold power. Year in and year out, it stayed in that same spot, only to be moved for dusting. Yet like most rebellious teenagers, I went through a phase when I disagreed with it entirely. After seventeen years, the words eventually found their way into my subconscious. Now, when something occurs that defies all explanation, I refer to these three words: "Jesus never fails."

Examples of this truth are found in every direction. Flip on any sporting event, and you are guaranteed to see stories of successful athletes who have overcome unfathomable hardships. Perhaps they lost a limb as a child or recovered from a life-threatening illness. Yet at the defining moment of their careers, they point toward the heavens to thank their Creator. With the fans cheering, cameras rolling, and microphones crowding their faces, they thank God for all He has done.

While our day-to-day examples may not be on such a public scale, we also have an opportunity to glorify God for what He has provided in our lives. Will you claim it was unbelievable or give Jesus the credit? Our Lord wants to be recognized, but it is not because He needs the acclaim. It is about aligning our hearts and mind with all He is doing through us. All things are possible for those who put their faith in Him.

Key Thought: What amazing things can you accomplish if you truly believe that Jesus never fails?

Additional Reading:
- "'For the word of God will never fail'" (Luke 1:37).
- "'What do you mean, *If I can?*' Jesus asked. 'Anything is possible if a person believes'" (Mark 9:23).
- "'O Sovereign Lord! You made the heavens and earth by your strong hand and powerful arm. Nothing is too hard for you'" (Jer. 32:17).
- "'I know that you can do anything, and no one can stop you'" (Job 42:2).

About The Author

IN STUDYING THE WORD OF God, Chris learns more about himself and the world around him. From the profound love of Jesus to the redemptive power of His mercy and grace, Chris writes to express the vast beauty of God's kingdom. Though his journey began as a personal one, Chris is honored to share his work with a worldwide audience.

Chris' greatest joy comes from encouraging others to deepen their relationship with Jesus. Whether in a sermon or written copy, his words are a testimony to what God has done in his life and what He can do for others as well.

As a writer, Chris will admit to sitting in front of a blank screen, praying for God's insight. Yet Jesus is always faithful and often infuses his mind with ideas that eventually become devotionals. As wonderful as these moments are, he finds even greater satisfaction in simply marveling at the Lord's creations in nature. It is this lifelong connection with God that inspires Chris to put pen to paper and share the wonders of our Father's majesty.

For more information
www.mindshiftministries.com
Email: chriscorradino@gmail.com

Ambassador International's mission is to magnify the Lord Jesus Christ and promote His Gospel through the written word.

We believe through the publication of Christian literature, Jesus Christ and His Word will be exalted, believers will be strengthened in their walk with Him, and the lost will be directed to Jesus Christ as the only way of salvation.

For more information about AMBASSADOR INTERNATIONAL please visit:

www.ambassador-international.com
@AmbassadorIntl
www.facebook.com/AmbassadorIntl

Thank you for reading this book!

You make it possible for us to fulfill our mission, and we are grateful for your partnership.

To help further our mission, please consider leaving us a review on your social media, favorite retailer's website, Goodreads or Bookbub, or our website.

More from Ambassador International

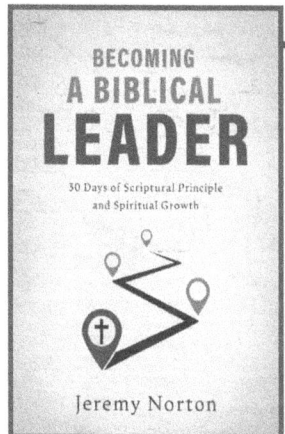

Pursuing biblically-driven personal growth is critical for the leader who desires to have an effective, God-centered ministry. *Becoming a Biblical Leader: 30 Days of Scriptural Principle and Spiritual Growth* beckons the reader to focus on one's calling as a biblical leader and offers thirty days of simple lessons and reflection as tools to experience the growth necessary to truly lead well.

Throughout the Bible, there are many references to the Christian life being compared to a ship. Whether we are floating along on calm seas or drowning in the waves of life, we are all in need of a sure Anchor for our souls. In *The Anchored Life: Nautical Principles that Help Believers Grow*, Marv Nelson and Tim Hibsman use nautical terms and analogies to show that the Bible is full of promises for the sea of life on which we are all sailing.

What does it mean to really live? Using Jesus' Sermon on the Mount as the blueprint, Martin Wiles answers some of the most pressing questions Christians have about effective Christian living. In this powerful work, Martin shares eighteen insights for learning how to pray, handle our anger, love our enemies, overcome worry, have a healthy marriage, and so much more. *Don't Just Live…Really Live* offers a practical approach for discerning how to live out the Bible in today's world.

www.ingramcontent.com/pod-product-compliance
Lightning Source LLC
Chambersburg PA
CBHW060534100426
42743CB00009B/1527